To
Pastor Sheree
— Wright

May my testimony
be a blessing
to you —

God Bless —
"Jackie"
Bishop Jackie

July 5, 2010

D1366277

The Hurt Lady

Spiritual Warfare Manual

For Individual or Group Study

Written by Bishop Jackie L. Green

Foreword by Lady Donna M. Du Bois

authorHOUSE®

AuthorHouse™
1663 Liberty Drive, Suite 200
Bloomington, IN 47403
www.authorhouse.com
Phone: 1-800-839-8640

This book is based on the true life testimony of the author. People, places, events are nameless to protect the privacy of actual persons, living or dead.

First published by AuthorHouse   2/23/2009

ISBN: 978-1-4389-3707-6 (sc)
ISBN: 978-1-4389-3708-3 (hc)

Printed in the United States of America
Bloomington, Indiana

This book is printed on acid-free paper.

Book contents may be used for research and references provided acknowledgement is given to the author.

The Author's Prayer for the Reader

As you open this book

I have already prayed for you

that the Spirit of God would draw you specifically

and bring the gift of salvation to you, bestow restoration upon you,

and bring reformation through you.

Dear Heavenly Father,

thank You for drawing this person to You through this book.

Save and set anyone free that is in bondage and needs liberty.

Bless everyone who purchases, promotes, translates, distributes,

teaches and reads

The Hurt Lady.

Let Your Holy Spirit fall upon the reader the moment their eyes look

upon the book

and the moment they touch the book cover.

Release to them a fresh impartation and increase of prayer and

intercession,

a greater love for God and one another,

a greater love and respect for women called by God,

and a spirit of wisdom and discernment of the times.

I bind up every critical, religious, traditional and demonic spirit

on assignment to hinder and confuse the reader

and to discredit the message of this book.

Let the eyes of the reader's understanding be opened and let

their hearts be flooded with the Light

of the Spirit of God and His Word.

I pray against all witchcraft assigned to curse this work,

and I decree that the power of God shall fall upon them

giving them space to repent and be saved

by the Blood and love of Jesus Christ.

Let Your Kingdom come, O God, and Your will be done in each

reader.

Let the angels of the Lord usher the message of this book

to denominations, nations and every generation.

Let women and girls be healed from every nation.

Let pastors and their wives be healed in every generation.

Let men and women ministers and lay persons be made whole

in every congregation.

In The Name of My Lord Jesus Christ I pray, AMEN.

This book is dedicated to
_____

Pastor's wives and Minister's Wives,

Women in Ministry and godly women who never

had a chance to publish their volumes of

experience in spiritual warfare...

some wounded,

some still in the fire,

some widowed,

some divorced and forgotten,

but still

STANDING.

Table of Contents

Acknowledgements

I want to thank the Lord Jesus Christ for all that was involved in my personal spiritual growth to birth this book. I owe the Lord all the honor and credit for this work being completed and published.

I want to acknowledge my husband, Pastor Anthony Green, for thirty five faithful years of marriage and team ministry. We have been through many seasons together and we still have a genuine love and respect for one another. By the grace of God and my husband's love, I can say I am now a "former Hurt Lady."

I want to take time to give special thanks to Pastor Brenda Davis, Prophet Cathy Fontenot, Deacon Carol Johnson and Sister Tiffany Bryant, my "Hub Team," for their prayers and world vision for this book and the Hurt Lady Conferences.

I also want to also thank a dear friend, Minister Miriam Perry, of Phoenix, Arizona, and my spiritual daughter, Dr. Crystal Banks, for another set of eyes, who also gave of their time in editing the manuscript and whose comments and insights were most valuable.

Endorsements for The Hurt Lady

"As a Pastor's wife and a woman in ministry, I give God glory for **The Hurt Lady**, **Spiritual Warfare Manual** , for the Preacher's wife. I thank God that He has released this writing through Bishop Jackie at a time where it is evident that a Pastor or Minister wife's life is not filled with glamour, but it is full of hurt and disappointment from her spouse, the congregation and other unseen forces. Bishop Jackie reminds us that the persecution, hurt and disappointments we experience as a spouse and as a woman in ministry comes with the calling; however, she points our focus to the Word of God where it commands us to take authority over the enemy. This anointed and timely book gives us the tools to fight the enemy as we walk in the calling God has placed on our lives. I am grateful to God that I am able to present a "**warfare guide**" to my spiritual daughters who are pastors, minister's wives and women in ministry. Praise be to God!"

Evangelist Charlezetta Nixon, First Lady
Brookins Community AME Church,
Los Angeles, California

"There is so much in these volumes of wisdom for many ages and stages in a woman's life. I would recommend this manual not only for preachers' wives and women in ministry, but for women--young and old-- who need to understand what God has ordained for them in intimate relationships. As a single woman in marketplace ministry in love with Jesus, the two chapters I found to be most resonant were: The Eight Hats of Deborah and Spiritual Mentors: A Remedy for the Hurt Lady. Through the spiritual mentoring Bishop Green has provided, so many women, and many spiritual warriors have walked through the journey from hurt to healed and are wearing many of those eight hats today. By the Blood of the Lamb and the word of her testimony, these warriors are ushering in God's Kingdom on earth! Bishop, God bless you for speaking life into women--and thus generations--everywhere through this work!"

Reverend Dr. Jannah Scott

Governor's Office, State of Arizona

Policy Advisor for Faith and Community Initiatives

Phoenix, Arizona

The Hurt Lady, as an updated and refined version of *Bricks Without Straw,* " is a testament to how we prophesy in part and how God gives more revelation as needed (in this case eighteen years later).

For this reason, I recommend **The Hurt Lady** to both new and seasoned Preachers' wives. I also highly recommend this manual to *women in* ministry who desire to break free of bondages and issues in their lives which block the flow of the anointing.

Elder Carolyn Anderson, First Lady
Living Water Ministries Church
Tucson, Arizona

"I must be honest. The title of this book was a turn off for me. My first reaction was, "I don't need to read about a Hurt Lady." However, as I began to open your book and read, the presence of God overshadowed me and I was truly touched by God. Bishop Jackie, your book is like a mirror magnified five times. The anointing on the written words in your book will "*shatter the glass houses*," of hurt and shame, that I and other women live in. There is healing on the pages of **The Hurt Lady**.

Prophet Meekness LeCato, Pastor
Shabach Word of Faith Christian Churchs
Phoenix, Arizona

"My goodness Bishop Jackie, I read the entire manuscript and could not put it down. I identified with so many of the chapters in the book and cringed when I read some of the PK hurts written so well by Elyzabeth. I unfortunately see how some have already labeled my daughter as a "mini-me" as she, at sixteen, leads in worship and holds leadership positions in the church. Having children that were "thrust" into the life of a PK, this book will give insight on how to communicate and pray with and over the children in a way I may not have ever seen. Because of your clarity and direct approach in your writing, I easily identified how Prince Charming had been assigned to me not only once but more than once. But for the grace of God and the teachings received under your ministry, I was set free and was able to discern the lovely and beautiful man of God I am now married to. I know I will spend some time when the book comes out writing and reflecting on my purpose statement. What a great tool that I can use along with prayer to find and check and recheck my balance as I maneuver the many positions God has purposed me for. This manual will help so many women: the walking wounded, the wounded who have stopped walking, and those who are being set up to walk into something they are not prepared for. What a great gift for engaged couples who may enter ministry! You have given me personally a way to reclaim my identity in Christ and the war manual to guard my marriage and children. I know this will be a book that Pastor David and I will have and really study together more than once."

I thank God for you.
Evangelist Shari Lyn Johnson, First Lady
Walker Chapel AME Church, Seattle, Washington

The Hurt Lady is an AWESOME all-in-one manual for Pastor's wives as well as women in ministry! It ministers to the total woman in either or both roles. As women we learn and adjust to what we are made to face and areas we find ourselves placed in. Bishop Jackie Green wrote this book encompassed with her own experiences and listening to the voice of the Lord, reaching the heart of every "HURT Lady." The tools that she gives are personalized for everyone in their own area of *hurt*. As you begin to read, and study this manual, the layers of *hurt* will begin to peel off and be replaced with the healing salve of God's Word! Just apply it! It's healing for your WHOLENESS!!!!

Pastor Cynthia Jackson, First Lady
Word of Life Miracle Deliverance Church
Brighton, Colorado

The Hurt Lady is a timely book in this hour. As God is removing the mask off the church and off of our culture, He has used Apostle Jackie Green to reveal what the true face of the church is to be. Shining in the pages of this comprehensive book is the reality of God's woman in her potential beauty, wisdom and power; fully integrated with God, the male gender, her family, local church and with the Body of Christ universally. **I was refreshed by the uncompromising truths** that will flow as a river of healing to many. I was impacted as I heard the Lord speak to my heart **"jugular vein."** He was referring to one of the two main veins that bring blood from the brain, back to the heart In other words the concepts in this book will strike a shocking blow to our way of thinking in the Body of Christ and will bring healing to our hearts and minds and make us one in Him and with one another. Thank you Jackie for this labor of love."

God's Daughter, Wife, Mother, Pastor
Prophet Esther Emmons
Life Christian Center and Prophetic Destiny Ministry, Johnstown, New York

"Dr. Jackie Green has skillfully and compassionately shared the revelation, truth and compassion of one who has intimate knowledge of the matters addressed in **The Hurt Lady.** As one who has received deliverance and healing from her wounds as a Hurt Lady, Dr. Green has poured herself out in a transparent manner, so that others may transition from hurt to wholeness; from being the walking wounded to being wholly healed warriors and Kingdom builders. She has clearly delineated the battle lines and the spiritual warfare waged against women in ministry. She has artfully and effectively communicated the strategies and tools needed for healing the hurts many of us have suffered in our journey as women in ministry. She speaks not as an outside observer but as a sympathetic and empowered "inside" battle-tested servant, who has survived and thrived, due to the saving grace of a powerful and compassionate Deliverer and Healer, Jesus Christ. **There is a powerful impartation** to be received from this timely work."

*Elder Dr. **Crystal M Banks, MD***
New Generation Christian Fellowship Church, Detroit, Michigan

The Hurt Lady acknowledges and addresses the silent cries, storms and abuse so many of our women suffer. Finally, our Deborahs, Esthers, Ruths and Annas can raise their heads and become the healed leaders they were destined to be. Accountability to our pastoral families in the churches is long overdue. This book not only identifies the "taboo" issues good church folk ignore, but offers a godly solution to recovery, restoration and redemption. For the sake of the generations to come, this is a must read for every minister's wife or woman in ministry whose calling has been silenced, buried or discounted. This book will also help anyone who is earnestly trying to deal with the overlooked bruises, emotional scars and double standards ignored by those in authority throughout the pulpits of America."

Elyzabeth Green
Daughter of Bishop Dr. Jackie Green
PK, Minister-in-Training and Police Officer
Second Baptist Church
Redlands, California

"Women in all facets of life need what God has given you in **The Hurt Lady**. Not only through personal experience, but He has given you the biblical tools to present this gift, to be used to deliver God's daughters from the clutches of the enemy via domestic violence, verbal and emotional abuse. I applaud you my sister in the Lord, for your courage to share the truth and allow God to use you to show His daughters there is a way up and a way out in the Lord." Love and victorious book signings.

Rev. Annetti Bullock, Associate Minister/Psalmist

Grace Bethel Missionary Baptist Church

Riverside, California

"I have enjoyed reading this very revelatory book. The **The Hurt Lady** is going to bring healing to many hurting women globally. This book has blessed me in many ways as a young Pastors wife, and as one who has a tremendous work to do in the earth for Jesus. The level of transparency in this book is awesome and I believe this is what is missing and is desperately needed in the Body of Christ for those women on the frontline in the natural and in the Spirit. There is much warfare that hurting ladies endure for their ministry as a wife, mother and woman in ministry; as a laborer/co-laborer. Those in ministry need the raw truth and love this book offers. Thank you so much for your sacrifice and obedience so that others may receive revelation to be healed and delivered by the power of the Blood of Jesus Christ."

Krystal Holland

Church Elder and Psalmist

New Generation Christian Fellowship Church

Phoenix, Arizona

"This book is incredibly honest in its portrayal of how godly women everywhere must deal with life's challenges. It is a call for women to "balance" themselves vertically and horizontally, whether we are in the pulpit or in the marketplace. Women in leadership who have been hurt, no matter what your title, will gain insight and encouragement from reading this book."

Carol E. Johnson, MSW, JD
Mitigation Specialist and Deacon
Maricopa County Office of the Public Defender
Phoenix, Arizona

"**The Hurt Lady** is the first book that was real, transparent, and would allow women to take off the mask they hide behind to cover up the hurt, pain, loneliness, secrets and shame. I believe if church women would take off the chains, shackles, and grave clothes we would see a transformation in the Body of Christ.   My life would be totally different if I had the teaching on "Beware of Prince Charming." Every single lady regardless of her age needs to be taught on this subject in order not to become a victim of the charmer whether in the church or outside of it. **The Hurt Lady** is a book that should be part of every lady's library."

Pastor Brenda E. Davis

Educator and Professional Counselor

Glendale Union School District

Assistant Pastor and Prophet

Phoenix, Arizona

"This Spiritual Warfare Manual on The Hurt Lady certainly enlarged my territory. For quite some time, Co-Pastor was in "name only" and in some areas it still is. Yet, through your manual, I found healing in that area. Yes, still there is work to be done in that area but I know it's going to take prayer and fasting. Your manual has ministered to me and answered all of my questions. My desire is to go back to school and establish the ministry God has given me. Thank you Bishop for your obedience and being a pioneering soldier. We're in it to win in Jesus' Name!"

Pastor "Glo" L. Broadous, First Lady

Calvary Baptist Church and

S.W.A.T. Ministries

Spiritual Warfare Against Trauma

Pacoima, California

Forward

Bishop Jackie Green, author of _The Hurt Lady, A Spiritual Warfare Manual for the Preacher's Wife (With Special Sections for Women in Ministry)_, gives valuable and much needed revelation and understanding about what she calls "real spiritual warfare in the parsonage." She discusses how this warfare affects the overall family and the spiritual and emotional health of women in the church, particularly Preacher's wives. There have been many books written about the stress of ministry on marriage, families and children, as well as places to go for professional help including doctors, psychiatrists, and psychologists. However to get to the root of the problem you must understand we are not fighting against flesh and blood but against principalities and powers. In this manual, Bishop Green exposes the emotional and spiritual battles that occur within marriages and families, including the struggles of Preachers' children. She gives you insight and the keys to the weapons of war to defeat the enemy in these areas.

Bishop Green states that, "Spiritual warfare transcends all ethnic and denominational barriers." In other words, Satan is not a respecter of persons and it has been his intent and mission from the beginning of time to destroy the 'nuclear' family. Nuclear comes from nucleus which means the center, the core, or the heart of something. Women represent the heart of life because they carry and nurture the seed. It does not matter what part of the world you live in, what church you are part of, or what title or position you hold: there is a battle occurring over your family with Satan, the father of lies and destruction.

The warfare in the parsonage begins with Pastors, their wives and their children where Satan wants to destroy the core or the heart of the church. If he can destroy the family, he can certainly destroy the church.

For women there is a strategic assignment to *keep us from being a force to bring balance in the church*. There is a battle to keep us hindered from nurturing our families and our church families into wholeness. A battle so destructive that it keeps us so oppressed that we become barren, unfruitful and unable to produce miracles of healing and deliverance through our intercession, and unable to nurture and produce healthy sons and daughters.

This manual by Bishop Green gives women who are married to pastors, married to ministers or generally in ministry, the insight and skills needed to stop the destruction of their marriages and families, and to bring healing and wholeness.

This manual is:

- *A life-line* for women who have been hurt in ministry to help them understand how to get free from the grasp of Satan in order to be healed and learn how to set others free.

- *A guide* to teach women how to be like Deborah; women who walk in the power and authority of God taking their rightful places as mothers of the church, as discerners of truth and as true worshippers.

- *A key* to unlock understanding of the New Testament principle of women being 'keepers of the home.' While giving insight into this principle, this book also gives women wisdom in how to balance their call to ministry while still being keepers of their homes.

As a pastor's wife, I have seen, experienced, and can relate to the warfare that occurs in the church. If you are a preacher's wife or a woman in ministry and need a life-line, you will be equipped through this manual with the keys you need to stand strong.

Thank you Bishop Green for writing this life giving manual for those of us…who are still standing! May your sensitivity, wisdom and insight in this book give women encouragement, hope and new life.

Lady Elect Donna M. Du Bois

Executive Elder

Judah International Ministries in Mackinaw, Illinois

Prophetic Preface

As I read **<u>The Hurt Lady,</u>** I was so blessed to once again experience in print what Bishop Green has lived and learned through her years of marriage, motherhood, and ministry. I have been one who has walked with her and seen first hand how she has overcome being a "Hurt Lady" to becoming a "Holy, Healthy and Happy Woman of God!

I believe that this is not just a book for WOMEN but MEN will also be set free from the mistakes and misunderstandings and misfortunes they may have had in dealing with the Hurt Lady. Many hurt ladies become "HARD" ladies, because they have been so wounded by words that they cover up their pains.

This book will surely set those free who read it.

Hear the Word of the Lord......

"Hurt Lady, Hurt Lady, no more to be sad

Hurt Lady, Hurt Lady, read and be so glad

Hurt Lady, Hurt Lady, I have heard your cries

Hurt Lady, Hurt Lady, you now can be set free from your past.

I have allowed this one to once be hurt, but it was part of the plan

because I knew she would be able to stand, and not fall in the sinking

sand! So to all who read this book, may this book be a mirror to show you

the real you, the hurt you, and the beauty that will come out of you.

Trust and know you have overcome the Hurt Lady and the Hurt Man

spirit, and you, too, will walk in love and forgiveness once again! Rejoice

and be glad for you have overcome by the Word of the testimony of this

woman of God and the Blood of the Lamb!"

And finally, **<u>The Hurt Lady</u>** is a picture of the *Hurt Church*, the Bride of Christ, that must be healed and cleansed of every spot and wrinkle. This prophetic book speaks to the very issues that the Church must deal with today in order to become one.

Prophet Cathy Fontenot
The Gathering Place
Palmdale, California

Introduction

"Christian women with hearts to serve God have been told that their unique gifts have no outlet, either in the church or on the front lines of ministry. When the Spirit of God has moved upon them to preach, they've been told to keep their mouths shut. When the Holy Spirit has nudged them to use their leadership gifts or their administrative anointings or their teaching abilities, they've been sent to a back room in the church to fix desserts for the Sunday night fellowship hour. When they've stepped out in faith to make a difference for the Kingdom of God through their careers, they've been rebuked for taking on "the man's role." It's time for the church to banish these prideful patriarchal attitudes. We must repent and call women out of the shadows and into the realm of authority God has ordained for all who follow the Savior." [1]

Does this sound like your life story? Well, I can certainly identify with these attitudes as a minister of the Gospel and a preacher's wife since I have been serving in that capacity now for over thirty years. Our stories all have something in common though we live in different parts of the world. We all had "expectations and experiences" put upon us and our families without full disclosure. Some of us made it, and some didn't. Some were casualties and some became callous and wounded. My prayer is that this spiritual warfare manual will help future generations of preacher's wives and women in ministry who may be wearing many hats but they can still recover from all the hurts.

I'm always looking for a good book that deals with the true to life story of how to be a wonderful minister's or pastor's wife or deals with the true journey of a woman in ministry. I've been successful in finding some good books, but most of them don't talk about the real "spiritual warfare in the parsonage." This manual was born out my hunger and thirst some twenty five years ago, when my husband and I were called to our first church. It is a revision of the first book in 1990, entitled "Bricks Without Straw." It was a small spiritual warfare manual that helped many pastors' wives and ministers' wives. Today, I thank God that I am able to build upon that and birth this new revised version. *This version is what I call an "amplified version" for it is expanded, increased and more complete.*

I am writing this manual as one that that has grown in spiritual authority, experience and grace. No matter what people

told me or how many books I read, I still had to grow in spiritual authority, experience and God's grace. The secret is being able to come out of it all, not bitter, but better.

Spiritual warfare transcends all ethnic and denominational barriers. Spiritual warfare comes with the territory of being a woman called to ministry. Twenty five years ago, no one told me about the warfare that would come against my marriage, my children and the ministry. But I want to tell my story so others will be better prepared than I was.

This manual is practical, and is written because God has taught my hands to war and my fingers to fight. With my hands, I have learned to worship and work the works of Him that has sent me. With my hands I have cooked and baked more meals that I care to mention for the weary travelers, unexpected guests and those that I have housed and fed at the parsonage. With my hands I have hugged and nursed my children and other folks children too, while caring for my husband and household. With my hands I have prayed and lifted many issues to heaven. I have laid my hands on the sick and they have recovered. With my fingers, I have written many books for the upbuilding of the kingdom, played many songs of worship and warfare on the keyboard, directed choirs and typed numerous sermons. I've pointed my finger in the Devil's face at least a million times and told him time and time again, "*No, I forbid you Devil, in Jesus Name.*"

I am thankful to my husband, Pastor Anthony Green for his years of faithfulness to God, to me, our children and to the church. I thank God for my children, our righteous seeds who are all young adults now, but serving God in various areas of creative ministry as God's modern day Levites.

Most of all I want to thank God that this book is a testimony *of a Hurt Lady that is now a healed lady.* I pray that this manual will set millions of women free that are *HURT LADIES*, that have been:

- hurt by their husbands
- hurt by their church
- hurt by denominations
- hurt by friendly fire
- hurt by poverty and lack
- hurt by religion and traditions of men
- hurt by domestic violence in the parsonage
- hurt by other women
- hurt by being misunderstood and neglected
- hurt by rejection
- hurt by sickness and infirmity
- hurt by her own self rejection

This book is for you. This book comes with the powerful love and compassion of the Savior, Jesus Christ. He was hurt too. And He understands "hurt" for He felt it upon the cross as He died for our sins. I dedicate this book to those hurt ladies, who can only be healed by the precious Blood of Jesus. Let your healing begin today, my sisters.

A Former Hurt Lady,
Bishop Dr. Jackie L. Green

Chapter 1

In the Beginning

Anthony and I met when I was in high school, and he was in his sophomore year at Bishop College. It was a divine connection, though neither one of us suspected we would one day be married and in ministry for life. God had plans for us to make a difference in our generation. It would be costly and it would require many hard decisions moving out of traditions to total transformation. By God's divine providence, I later went to Bishop College in Dallas, Texas and the rest is history.

In the beginning, we were young, naïve, courageous and committed to Christ. We had been married just ten years when we were called to our first pastorate. We went there with two small children at the time, and we had served under three pastors in three cities; Rochester, New York, Washington, D.C. and Phoenix, Arizona.

We had some knowledge of the inner workings of the pastorate but very little in spiritual warfare.

It's important how a marriage and ministry begin. It usually sets the tone for the years to come. The first few years of marriage are foundational years or the root years and anything that is not corrected before the foundation is laid remains in the foundation. It can be corrected if you are both willing to go back to the foundation and rip it open and pull out those things and reset the foundation. This can be costly and requires a lot of work. Most couples are not willing to do it. They would rather not rock the boat but choose to go with the flow.

The first years of our marriage and ministry began in seminary. My husband wanted to go right from his undergraduate studies and work on his Master of Divinity. This meant that both of us could not go to school. I opted to stop school for a season and support him by working full time, helping him with his projects and papers and even assisting him at the church where he did his field work. I had a strong calling on my life also, but was willing to wait and help him obtain his goal. Once this goal was obtained, our hope was that he would be a prime candidate for a pastoral position. People ask me how did my marriage last through the years?

Sacrifice is one of the first prerequisites for a successful marriage and ministry. Sacrifice was in the foundation of our marriage and ministry. We would not be together today without this component. After 35 years of marriage, it is still a major part of our marital and ministry success. It is a weapon of warfare that Satan's kingdom cannot comprehend.

As my husband pursued his seminary studies, I worked full time as most seminary wives had to do. I remember the wives coming together for "gripe sessions" and not prayer sessions, to talk about how hard life was treating us. The fantasy was that some day our husbands would be called to a big church and these days of poverty and hard times would soon be over. All the while, no one was preparing us (the wives) for the inevitable warfare that was awaiting us and really was already in motion in seminary. We were destined for spiritual conflict. There was no combat training in seminary. There was no spiritual warfare training for the conflicts we would face that could literally destroy our marriages and ministries overnight. Many marriages were destroyed before they left seminary.

I want to encourage the wives of seminarians to find a strong prayer and intercession group of women. Also it is important to find out what God has called you to do and not put your calling on a shelf. If you think that your husband's ministry will not affect you, or that it's just his calling and not yours, you are being deceived. Satan will use you to sabotage your own ministry by your words, unspoken vows and actions, because **your denial** of "team ministry and team work" will be the entry point to spiritual attacks.

When my husband finally finished seminary, I remember saying, "Well, these bean and cornbread days will soon be over. We can buy a nice car, a house, save some money, start a family, and really get ahead. I can go back to school now. We can live like normal people."

I learned the hard way that we (preacher's wives) were not like everyone else. We were called by God and we had an arch enemy. Little did I realize that the road would get harder. Not because we did anything wrong or because we were sinful, but because the mantles on our lives brought with them powerful warfare. For us to be successful, we needed more than a seminary degree. We would have to become skilled warriors in the Spirit, otherwise, we would never reach our full potential.

If someone had whispered in my ear, "Honey, you'll still be eating some beans and cornbread even when he pastors," I would have never believed them. I was too young, too naïve and inexperienced in spiritual warfare. I needed a spiritual mentor. A seasoned woman who had been there, done that. I realized years and years later that deciding to follow Jesus is not a normal life. Yes, a doctor's wife or a lawyer's wife can easily expect his years of training to kick in and net a hundred thousand a year or more. But the minister's wife and pastor's wife, even with a seminary trained husband, might get a great salary or no salary. He might get benefits or no benefits at all. **There was no guarantee on anything except that GOD WAS WITH US.** I am not saying that God does not desire that we have abundance, but I am saying we are not to equate success in ministry with material things. God promised us that he would be "with us" and supply our needs. Sometimes what we think we need is not a need, but a want or a comparison to what other ministries have. Learning to be content with what God has planned for our lives goes a long way.

"Don't love money. Be satisfied with what you have. For God has said, I will never fail you. I will never abandon you." Hebrews 13:5 (NLT)

"So if we have enough food and clothing, let us be content."
I Timothy 6:8 (NLT)

"Not that I was ever in need, for I have learned how to be content with whatever I have. I know how to live on almost nothing or with

5

everything. I have learned the secret of living in every situation, whether it is with a full stomach or empty, with plenty or little. For I can do everything through Christ, who gives me strength." Philippians 4:11-13 (NLT)

I was not ready for years and years of sacrifice and I was disappointed with the fruit of many years of sacrificing for my husband and the church. Disappointment opened the door to deep hurt and a bitter root began to grow and wrap itself around my heart. I was hurting also because I could not seem to find contentment and be satisfied with what I had. Every hurt has an entry point. If these hurts are not traced back to the entry point and dealt with, they will continue to grow and poison our spirit man.

I learned years later that "God will not forget our sacrifices and labor of love for the Kingdom." (Hebrew 6:10) He will honor every woman that has honored her husband and sacrificed for the Kingdom's sake. I understand now that God gives every pastor's wife and minister's wife "a special grace" to stand with that man and to serve those people. If not for the grace, we would have no pastor's wives left to testify. If you can walk in that "special grace," it will prevent you from becoming hurt and bitter. For in that special grace are powerful ingredients called "peace, contentment and forgiveness."

(Photo from Redlands Daily Facts Newspaper, 1983, Redlands, California)

Pastor Anthony Green and First Lady Jackie Green in 1983 with two young children (Elyzabeth and Joel) as they began their first pastorate. Like most clergy couples, with great hopes and dreams for the future they would have to have "on the job" spiritual warfare training. By God's grace they did not become a casualty and survived to testify of God's victory in their lives and legacy 25 years later.

If you are just beginning as a pastor's wife or minister's wife, here are a few wisdom keys to lessen your hurts, wounds and disappointments in ministry.

REFLECTION AND PRAYER

TEN HURT PREVENTION WISDOM KEYS

1.   Never lay down your personal vision for ministry and marriage to neglect your gifts and calling.

2.   Connect to spiritual women in Christ that know how to pray and intercede.

3.   Set realistic expectations for ministry.

4.   Ask God for a mentor or spiritual mother to help you through the beginning years.

5.   Spend time in prayer with your husband. Even though he is studying in seminary, make sure you are growing with him.

6.   Begin to read and study on spiritual warfare. Most seminaries don't even teach or believe in spiritual warfare, demons or witchcraft.

7.   Pray and seek the Lord for the spirit of wisdom and the grace

to walk with your husband as his wife and helpmate.

8.   Get deliverance prayer for areas of hurt, disappointments and wounds. Seek out those that are more mature and can pray for you in those vulnerable areas.

9.   Don't compare your marriage or ministry with others. Let God do a unique thing in you and be content with what God is doing with you.

10. Spend daily time with God in His Word and prayer. This will keep you in tune with what God is saying. Be your husband's number one intercessor.

Chapter 2

The Eight Hats of Deborah

"Deborah, a wife of Lappidoth, was a prophet, who was judging Israel at the time. She would sit under the Palm of Deborah, between Ramah and Bethel in the hill country of Ephraim, and the Israelites would come to her to settle their arguments/disputes." Judges 4:4-5

"There were no warriors in Israel until I, Deborah, arose."
Judges 5:7   (Every Day Bible)

As I studied the text in Judges 4 and 5, it is clear that Deborah had the anointing upon her life in eight areas. Like many pastor's wives, minister's wives, female co-pastors and women in ministry, Deborah had to wear many hats and fulfill many positions. She was a woman first, wife, Mother of Israel (spiritual mother), Judge, Prophetess, Military Strategist (General), National Leader and Worshipper. God has equipped most women with the ability to do multiple things "well." What a gift for any man of God that has a wife filled with the Spirit of God, Spirit led and multi-tasked.

The first hat Deborah wore was her "womanhood." As women of God no matter what God calls us to do, we must never try to be a "man." We are a "womb man, beautiful and feminine, incubator, nurturer, helpmate and suitable intellectual companion." We are fearfully and wonderfully made. And I am sure Deborah kept herself beautiful inside and out. She was attractive to her husband and she was pleasant to look upon. As women of God we must remain "feminine." Feminine means "womanly, female, ladylike, gentle, soft, delicate, and of the female gender." But Deborah first and foremost was a woman and was not apologetic for her gender. Her gender did not hinder her being used by God on many levels of leadership and He even placed her over a nation.

"Deborah was a woman, but God did not give her oversight because of that. She was a woman of distinction. A woman of righteousness. A woman that God could use. And that is why God uses any leader. They must be righteous, and in right relationship with Him first of all." 2

12

Deborah did not allow her womanhood be an excuse for not being used in higher levels of leadership in Israel, and neither did her husband, Lappidoth.

That leads us into the second hat of Deborah. She was a Wife. She was married and therefore was submitted to her husband and had to take care of a home also. We do not know if she had natural children, but she probably did if she was not barren. The Bible does not tell us. The fact that there is no indication in Scripture that her husband was against her calling is a testimony in itself. Deborah came up during a time that oppression of women in the Old Testament was at its height. Women were property and had no voice. But Deborah's husband did not allow her voice to be silenced. What a man of God he must have been! Praise God for those husbands that will "not clip the wings of their wives" that have a calling of God. Deborah's husband Lappidoth allowed Deborah to be the overseer that God has called her be. When Deborah was home, she was Mrs. Lappidoth. But when Deborah went to her Oval Office, under the Palm Tree of Deborah, she was the Chief Justice of the Supreme Court of Israel. It is important to find the balance between marriage and ministry, but it can be done. Deborah is our example. Deborah is our "she-roe" and success story that women can do ministry and flow with their husband. Husbands and wives are great teams.

Deborah was first secure in being a woman and secondly secure in her marriage. These are keys for the First Lady and minister's wife. And even women in ministry must not let their gender disqualify them. Women of God must flow with their husbands and pray that their husbands are not insecure in their callings.

The third hat of Deborah was the call to arise be a "Mother in Israel." One of the positions of a pastor's wife is a "spiritual mother." Deborah arose as a Mother in Israel and took on the mantle to nurture, protect and guard her nation. She was one that birthed new levels of righteousness and victory for the nation. She birthed a standard of righteousness. SHE NURSED THE NATION BACK TO WHOLENESS. Pastor's wives have to be able to nurse the congregation back to wholeness, especially among the women and girls. She is a mother to many teenagers. Deborah was there for a young generation coming up to see what true mothering looked like on a national level. She was a Mother in Israel and ruled for 40 years. "There was peace in the land for forty years."
Judges 5:31b (NLT)

The fourth hat that Deborah wore was the Judge. As I said earlier, she would be considered today as the Chief Justice of the Supreme Court. The Bible says that the nation came to her to have all their disputes settled. She sat in judgment to execute sentences and to minister justice. She had to have the Spirit of Wisdom upon her life. The Spirit of Wisdom alone qualifies one to be a strong leader for the people of God. It is the principle thing, get wisdom. I don't know if Deborah would have been like "Judge Judy" whom we see on television today, but she was I am sure a woman to be dealt with. She ruled her courtroom well. Deborah ruled under the palm tree daily. Every pastor's wife needs discernment and the ability to judge all things fairly.

Fifthly, Deborah was a Prophetess. This office of the prophet Deborah walked in was powerful and necessary for the day she lived in. Many pastor's wives have a prophetic calling on their lives. Even the gift of prophecy is very needed in the church today and must be exercised with balance and wisdom. Imagine having Supreme Court judges that are prophets of the Lord. How different America would be today! Deborah also walked in the office of a prophet in her day and was able to articulate the Voice and message of God to the people. She also was able to war against principalities and powers that kept Israel in bondage and rebellion and defied the law of God. Deborah had the "eye of the seer" and could discern and hear the Voice of God for the nation. *She was a national voice, a national visionary, and a prophet to the nation.* She was well known among the heathen nations as well as God's mouthpiece, and I believe like, the true prophets of old, she was feared by the pagan nations.

The sixth hat that Deborah wore was the "Military Strategist. She was a General. She operated the command post of Israel, and Barak was her right hand man. He was wise enough to recognize the mantles on Deborah's life that overrode the fact that she was a woman. Barak saw a military general. One that was skilled in the art of war, skilled in the conduct of war and executing plans against the enemy. Deborah controlled the military forces. Hear the conversation between General Deborah and Barak:

" *One day she sent for Barak son of Abinoam, who lived in Kedesh in the land of Naphtali. She said to him, "this is what the Lord, the God of Israel, commands you: Call out 10,000 warriors from the tribes of Naphtali and Zebulun at Mount Tabor. And I will call out Sisera, commander of Jabin's army, along with his chariots and warriors, to the Kishon River. There I will give you victory over him." Barak told her, "I will go, but only if you go with me" Judges 4:7-8 (NLT)*

Was Barak a wimp? I don't think so. Barak was wise and recognized that Deborah was anointed, appointed, and an able General of God's armies. Barak trusted the military strategist that

God had put in Deborah. You see when you go to war and you are on the battlefield, it doesn't matter if you are male or female. In the military both are soldiers and both bleed red blood. Both have laid their lives on the line and soldiers are not concerned that the soldier beside them is male or female, but they are concerned that that soldier is skilled in the art of war and skilled in the use of their weapon. Deborah was an overseer of Israel and she was **skilled in war,** and the nation of Israel looked up to her.

The seventh hat Deborah wore was that of a National Leader, one in high profile for forty years. She was a national figure and had to balance that with trying to have a private life with her husband. As a "national overseer" she had to learn to balance times in private with those times in public. She had to deal with criticism and bad press just like national figures today. She had women haters and men haters for sure. She had to deal with stress! Thank God she was a true Worshipper!

Finally, the eighth hat that Deborah wore was a true Worshipper.

"On that day Deborah and Barak son of Abinoam sang this song:
"Israel's leaders took charge, and the people gladly followed. Praise the
Lord! Listen, you kings! Pay attention, you mighty rulers! For I will sing

to the Lord. I will make music to the Lord, the God of Israel. Wake up, Deborah, wake up! Wake up, wake up, and sing a song! Arise, Barak! Lead your captives away, son of Abinoam! Judges 5:1-3, 12 (NLT)

Deborah was a true Worshipper and knew how to praise and worship God! She knew how to give God the credit for the battles she won. She would not touch the gold nor the glory of God! That is the true heart of an overseer. We must not touch the money dishonestly and we must not take the credit for ourselves. It sounds like Deborah had integrity and intimacy with God. She was a singer and a praiser. Her name is listed first before Barak's in scripture which gives her preeminence in the leadership role. The *Song of Deborah* is not the "Song of Barak." Barak joined in the song, but the song came up out of Deborah's heart and soul. She was a Psalmist or singing Prophet of the Lord. She was a strong intercessor and she loved the Voice and the Law of God.

As I looked at these eight hats that Deborah wore, I asked the question that most women want to know. When did she have time to fry chicken and clean her house? When did she have time to get her nails manicured and her hair done? Did she take a vacation? Well, in Deborah's day surely she took some time off for herself in order to be able to oversee Israel faithfully for 40 years. Surely she raised up sons and daughters and other leaders to carry on some

of the work. Surely she and Lappidoth went away and spent time

together with the family. She was a wise woman of God and she

knew from worshipping the Lord that "she was not the Christ." She

drew her strength from the Lord. She stayed under the shadow of

the Almighty and drew from the wellspring of salvation. Deborah

knew that Yahweh was her all and all. Pastor's wives and minister's

wives and women in ministry can use Deborah's life as a example

in staying balanced, beautiful and bold for God! **DEBORAH

COULD BALANCE BECAUSE SHE SPENT AMPLE TIME

IN THE SECRET PLACE WITH GOD. SHE WAS A TRUE

WORSHIPPER. BALANCE COMES FROM BOWING BEFORE

THE KING!**

The spiritual warfare that Deborah had is still the same level of

warfare that we have today. Deborah didn't have the support system

that women have today, nor the revelation we flow in today. But

Deborah did not let the "gender war" stop her. She came up in hard

times. I am encouraged when I read about her and understand that I

can do more than she did. If she wore all those hats back then, surely

we can survive with the few hats we wear today. I want to examine the

"Gender Warfare." When we understand where the war came from and

that we fight not against flesh and blood but the same old principalities and powers that Deborah warred against.

A Poem

Deborah's Conversation with God ₃

Deborah had a conversation with God one night.

And she didn't tell anyone right then of her new destiny and plight.

God called her do what tradition and history said was "only for men."

God doesn't need our permission to select His leaders now or back then.

Deborah didn't debate with God for long about her new assignment or her gender.

God chose a woman because it pleased Him and it served His purpose;

and also to make sure the religious folk would always remember.

God said to Deborah, "I have chosen you to judge and speak for Me,

and be a "Mother" to a whole nation of My people to help them see.

That includes the stiffnecked, the religious, and the hating women too.

Deborah told her husband Lappidoth, who probably scratched his head.

He smiled, and said, "My woman is chosen by God,

and I'm gonna protect her against those that will resist being "female led.""

So Deborah stepped up and arose for forty years.

She ruled under the anointing, authority and audacity of God,

amid hard times and tears.

She was the talk of the town for 40 years as she led,

but for sure all her accusers would one day be silenced or dead.

To this day, men and women try to deny her authority and discredit her

gender,

As a judge and prophet, and even elevate Barak over her instead.

Even today God never chooses or calls His leaders by their gender

or by their outward appearance, but He looks at the heart.

When will we get that through our heads?

© 2006, Written by Bishop Dr. Jackie L. Green

12 Reasons the Body of Christ Fights Women in Leadership and in Partnership with Men 4

1. **The Fall of Mankind** -Satan in the Garden of Eden attacked Eve and caused her to   sin against God and Adam also fell. A curse came into being. (Genesis 3:15)

2. **The Spirit of Misogyny** - A demonic spirit in the world that hates women and has brought worldwide oppression upon women and girls, especially by causing women to hate themselves and their gender. This world ruler spirit is alive and well today.

3. **The Spirit of Male Chauvinism** - A demonic spirit that causes men to be blinded to the God given value of the female and Godly purpose of women in the earth. This spirit is an abusive and oppressive spirit over women/girls and it releases demonic submission.

4. The Spirit of Religion and Tradition - A strong demonic spirit assigned to the Church and society to put laws and regulations above relationship with God and one another. The spirit of tradition keeps alive the old mindsets of the forefathers and will not accept the move of the Holy Spirit; nor, is this spirit open to admit it is in error or admit that there is a better way. It refuses to give women any credibility, access or the same opportunities men have in the Body of Christ.

5. Wrong or Limited Interpretation of Scripture - For thousands of years, by various denominations and those males in leadership, scripture was abused and misinterpreted to enforce the oppression of women. Women have also misinterpreted what God is doing and hate themselves and other women, that are advancing the Kingdom.

6. Insecure Husbands and Insecure Male Leadership

7. Jealous and Insecure Women in the Church

8. Denominational /Doctrinal Differences

9. Greed and self glory – Mammon and the control and distribution of wealth in the earth by greedy men, has kept women in bondage and poverty.

10. Spirits of Confusion - Demonic spirits stirring up confusion

11. Spirits of Division - A demonic spirit assigned at The Fall of Man in the Garden that works divisiveness and schism in the Church and the State.

12. Witchcraft - Infiltration in the church by ministers of Satan, witches, and warlocks on assignment to keep the Church from maturing and coming into unity, Kingdom authority and fulfilling the Great Commission.

REFLECTIONS AND PRAYER

Which one of these tactics is Satan fighting you with today? List them here. God is calling you to pray and fight with the spiritual weapons of warfare and to overcome the tactics of the enemy as Deborah did. Write a full page here as you reflect on the eight hats of Deborah and the hats you are wearing.

Chapter 3

Know Your Position

"We will not win the future war of the Church without women coming into place for what God is doing in this hour. Now is the time, dear sisters, for you to understand your invaluable worth, to come into the alignment God has for you and to exercise the unique gifts and calling the Lord has for you at this strategic time in history. If you will do so, great victory lies ahead for the Church of Jesus Christ." 5

As women of God embarking upon the task of being a helpmate for our husbands and our Pastor, I would like you to consider my thirteen suggestions for being positioned this hour. Minister's wives have a lot on their plates, but one thing is for sure, she must know her position in Christ, her position in marriage, her position in the church and her position in the larger Body of Christ. Alignment is very important not only for her to be effective, but for those that are clinging and drawing from her. Alignment literally means the proper positioning or state of adjustment; to be in a state of agreement or cooperation among persons, groups, nations, etc., with a common cause or viewpoint. So many women of God has been hurt and wounded because they are not properly aligned and they are not in positions that God has called them to. We must get aligned and positioned in the Kingdom this hour. Being positioned and aligned has been difficult because the preacher's wife has had to wear so many hats and masks.

"No school, no seminaries have offered courses that provide her for the responsibilities she would face. Her identity has been largely based on images assigned to her by local congregations. She has been assigned the roles of public-relations servant, mission and education leader, musician, assistant pastor and leader of fashions. Whether she has sought to perpetuate any or all of these roles, she has nonetheless, felt the pressure to conform and to be what the congregation felt she should be. In so doing, her real creative initiative has been lost and her right to choose the course her life would take has been blocked. The day has come when this condition need **no longer** prevail." 6

1. KNOW YOUR SPIRITUAL POSITION IN CHRIST

Firstly, the Pastor's wife and minister's wife is seated with Christ in heavenly places. She is one that is not below, but above and walking in the things of the Spirit. **She is not a novice, or beginner, but she is mature and Spirit filled and Spirit led!** She is able to discern and recognize that God has given her "spiritual positioning." She must not be carnal and fleshy. She holds a front line battle position whether she wants to or not. It is not a pew or bench position or a title holding position. It is a front line battle position in the spirit realm. If she is not skilled in spiritual warfare, she could open the door to defeat and death upon her own household. She has a key spiritual position in prayer and intercession and spiritual warfare. **She is a spiritual guard for her husband, children and the church. She is a watchman on the wall. She is one that must have eyes to see in the spirit realm.**

2. KNOW YOU HAVE BEEN POSITIONED TO LEAD

She has a pacesetter position. The congregation uses her as a thermometer for worship and righteousness, to set a standard. She is a standard bearer. She and her husband set the tone for worship by allowing the people to flow in the Spirit of liberty. For where the

Spirit of the Lord is, there is liberty. The women will for sure follow her lead in dress, hair style, in ministry, marriage and motherhood. They will copy her therefore she must be a godly example in all things.

3. KNOW YOUR POSITION AMONG OTHER WOMEN

She is an original. She is not only the "First Lady," she is the ONLY LADY." The term First Lady is a term of endearment, but Jezebel is always contemplating how she can become the "Second or Next Lady. The Pastor's wife brings particular gifts and callings to the ministry along with her husband. Many things they will do together as a couple. Other times, she will flow in her unique giftings that will be a blessing to the Body. She is a gift to the church and the Body of Christ. There is a grace upon her life to "influence" others on many levels. Her uniqueness above all the other women in the church can bring additional warfare of jealousy and strife. She has to know how to walk in that place of "First Lady" and not have her wings clipped by traditions and "women's ministry trauma/drama." She should not be original because she is wearing the biggest hat. But she is original because God has called her make a greater impact on women and girls in her sphere of influence. She will also have a profound effect on the men in the church and her sons. They will look to her as a role model for all the other women in the church, and even her sons will use her as a standard when it is time to find their wives.

4. KNOW YOU ARE A SPIRITUAL MOTHER

She is a spiritual mother, mentor and midwife to many. Because of her godly example and influence, there is a dimension of spiritual mothering that begins to come to the forefront. Spiritual mothering can be with both male and females. She should be able to impart wisdom, wise counsel, discernment, holiness, faith, obedience, divine order, love and kindness, correction/rebuke, and prophetic insight. She should be one that flows in the **discerning of spirits and** able to counteract any spirits of error and rebellion that would arise in the camp. As a spiritual midwife to both men and women, she will help them birth forth their gifts, visions, and callings. She will also birth the heart and purposes of God in prayer and travail on behalf of others and the church.

5 . KNOW YOU ARE A CO-LABORER

She is a co-laborer and team player. She should be in team ministry with her husband, not necessarily to the same degree, but to the degree that she can balance marriage, home life and ministry.

As a team player, "hospitality" becomes a major part of her duties while being on the team with her husband. Raising the children and speaking into their lives and pulling out of them their gifts and callings becomes a full time job. As a team player, she also balances being wife and lover and protects their intimacy and keeps him accountable to his commitments to honor and cherish her. Her ministry duties will vary according to the ages of the children and her personal responsibilities to the pastor as wife, lover and friend.

6. KNOW YOU ARE YOUR SISTER'S KEEPER

She is her "sister's keeper." There are many pastor's wives and minister's wives that need another sister in their same position or rank to network and bond with. Minister's and pastor's wives need confidants and prayer partners to help them on this journey. It is not easy when a minister's wife is isolated, frustrated and wounded. God has set particular pastor's wives in the Body to mentor others and to network support groups, conferences and counseling. This is a very important position. It requires experience, wisdom and nurturing skills as well as spiritual maturity. I began having seminars and conferences also to make sure my sisters were getting support and prayer in the region. *"I am my sister's keeper"* meaning, I look out for her; I care about her; I love and protect her; I speak truth to her; I hold her accountable; and I don't betray or wound her.

7. KNOW YOU HAVE POWER AND AUTHORITY

She is in a position of spiritual authority. Pastors and ministers wives titles are inherited. If your spouse is a clergy, you inherit their lifestyle and warfare. You also inherit spiritual authority that you may or may not be trained for. Demons don't care whether you have spiritual warfare training or not. They begin their program of destruction as soon as you take your position as First Lady, and you had better know how to discern and pull down the strongholds of the enemy. Ignorance of spiritual things hinders you from walking in spiritual authority. Being the wife of a pastor is being the wife of someone that is in a five fold ministry office. With every office comes rights and responsibilities and new enemies. It is important that she seek the Holy Spirit to help her understand her spiritual authority through His Word, prayer and fasting and through mentorship. **She must learn to execute spiritual authority in Jesus' Name, His Word and His Blood over rebellion, error, demons, witchcraft and seduction spirits and spirits of sabotage sent to the her marriage, ministry and motherhood (children).**

8. KNOW YOUR OWN CALLING, PURPOSE AND DESTINY

She should know her calling or position in the church and in the Body of Christ. Many pastors wives and ministers wives do not know their own calling, spiritual gifts or placement in the Body of Christ.   They only see themselves as the wife of the Pastor, but they are ignorant and fearful of their destiny in Christ. Many are hindered by denominational, gender and traditional barriers and therefore do not develop their own giftings. When this happens, abuse and hurts can take place easily. When a pastor's wife or minister's wife does not know their purpose and destiny in Christ, they are not fitly joined in that church or the Body of Christ. They must seek the Lord and the Pastor needs to make sure she is properly placed in the church. How sad to have a gift in your midst that is never unwrapped or recognized.

9. KNOW THE VALUE OF TAKING CARE OF YOURSELF AND LOOKING YOUR BEST. DRESS FOR THE DAY.

She is on display 24-7. We are on display whether we like it or not. It comes with the profession. We are to look good first because we represent the King of Kings. We are His ambassadors. Secondly, we are to look good for our husbands. We are never to become haggard and poor in our appearance. We represent our husbands. Finally, we represent the people of God that we serve in the community and in the world. We must keep our appearance up. It is part of our positional duty as an ambassador and representative for the Kingdom of God. Many times in the governmental arena, when women are promoted to offices, they have to get a whole new wardrobe and they have to dress the part. I am not advocating "out dressing" other women, but I am advocating excellence in our dress and modesty too. It is important for our husbands to keep us well dressed, our hair done and demonstrate his care for his wife and children.

I was never a pastor's wife that was into the "hat thing." But to each his own. I was and still am a conservative dresser but always mindful to "dress for the day," for I don't know where the Master will have me represent Him that day. You may be "going through" as a pastor's wife, but you don't have to look like it. An excellent appearance is very important and it will also keep you from walking in low self esteem. Your appearance is part of your positioning and alignment.

10. KNOW YOUR "EQUAL" POSITION AMONG MEN.

She is equal to any man in God's eyes. This is key this hour as women in all walks of life have been taught and heard gender bias and wrong interpretations of scripture to keep women bound. Though some men may still disrespect us, we must know who we are in Christ and that there is neither male nor female in the Kingdom of God. We must not be intimidated by gender prejudice, but we must re-teach false doctrine as it relates to women and we must model a balance ministry team with our husbands. We must know our equal position among men, so that we can pass it on to our sons and daughters.

"Galatians 3:28 says that in Christ "there is neither Jew nor Greek, slave nor free, male nor female. (NIV). In other words, when we are "in Christ," and when the Holy Spirit is operating through human vessels, gender distinctions become irrelevant. God works through human agents, whether men or women, to accomplish His purposes. He doesn't look on the outward appearance; He look at the heart to see if the image of His Son is evident." 7

11. KNOW THAT YOU NEED ACCOUNTABILITY

She needs someone to keep her in check. It is important to be accountable first to God, second to your spouse if you are married, and to other spiritual leadership that will speak truth to you so you will be balanced. We need to submit to those that have proven integrity and who will speak truth to us when we are hurt and wounded, or when we need correction. **WE ARE NEVER ABOVE CORRECTION.** Correction is not rejection from God or those in authority. Even as pastors and pastor's wives, we still need someone that we can go to for advice and correction. This is a part of the balance that is lacking and that is so needed in the Body of Christ today.

12. KNOW YOUR TIMES AND SEASONS IN THE LORD

She must be a "now" woman. We must be women in the "know" of what God is doing in our midst and in the Body of Christ. We must be "now woman" in order to be positioned proper like the Tribe of Isaachar, who knew the times and seasons of the Lord, in their lives and in nation of Israel. We may be serving in a local church, but our destiny is bigger than the local church. We must remember that we are connected to a tremendous network of believers and we must be in sync with what God is doing on a global level. Therefore we must increase our discernment and pray for the gift of discerning of spirits. Do not get distracted with daily trauma and drama that seems to have no end and can drain you. Have an ear to hear what the Spirit of the Lord is saying, and be able to shift with Him in your life and ministry. So many women of God are "stuck" because they didn't obey the Voice of the Lord and shift into their new season. You may be a pastor's wife now, but in the next season you could be ordained and serving in an assistant pastor role. Be open to change, for it is one sure way we know we are growing. *Be a "now woman" and not a "later woman." You could miss out on what God is doing personally and corporately.*

13. KNOW YOUR POSITION IN THE BEDROOM .

She is the only one that should satisfy her husband. This is an area that many pastor's wives and minister's wives and women in ministry must guard. We get so busy and even religious that we do not minister to our own husband's sexual needs and desires for intimacy. A verse that I framed and put in our bedroom for many years is found in Proverbs *5:18-19.* It was a constant reminder of the importance of nurturing our intimacy. It was also a prophetic declaration against the entrapments of the enemy that are sent to both the Pastor and wife to defile the marriage bed and destroy intimacy.

"May your fountain be blessed, and may you rejoice in the wife of your youth. A loving doe, a graceful deer— may her breasts satisfy you always, may you ever be captivated by her love." (NIV)

Close any gaps or open doors to the enemy in your private chambers. Enough said on that.

REFLECTION AND PRAYER

Take time to pray over those thirteen areas of positioning. Ask the Lord to strengthen you and bring revelation on each one of them. Write out your life purpose statement with scripture. Keep it before you and see how God will cause you to reach your full potential in Him. List also your spiritual gifts. List your three greatest obstacles that keep me from being properly positioned.

My Life Purpose Statement

Scriptures to support my Life Purpose Statement

My spiritual gifts are:

My three greatest obstacles that keep me out of position:

Chapter 4

Balancing Singleness, Marriage, Motherhood and Ministry

"Satan hates women, single or married; motherhood and ministry. Satanic interference makes balancing even more frustrating. In faith and sometimes in fatigue, we try to balance home and church, marriage and motherhood, singleness and ministry, the workplace and all the unspoken expectations of the church. But I am convinced that there is a special grace and wisdom upon women of God to balance all these dimensions and not have a nervous breakdown." 8

Balanced in Singleness
"Singleness is not a curse, it's a privilege."

I want to address the *single woman* in ministry that may or may not be parenting and deal with some of their areas of hurt. As a senior pastor, I want to say first of all to single women in leadership, "don't waste your singleness." Singleness has its advantages. Jesus our Lord was single and He didn't waste anytime saying "O woe is me because

I'm single." He was taking care of His Father's business.   According to the Apostle Paul, singleness is a privilege and it is a place that you can totally devote yourself to the Lord, and it is a place that does not have the distractions that married life brings. There is a freedom you can experience being single that you will not have being married. After all, it is important to note here that everyone is not called nor are they destined to be married. The "ministry of marriage" is not for everyone. So, I want to encourage and applaud those that are walking out their singleness and that are not divided emotionally or spiritually in their singleness, but they have found wholeness and purpose.The Apostle Paul lived a single life in the ministry and says to us:

"I want you to be free from the concerns of this life. An unmarried man can spend his time doing the Lord's work and thinking how to please him. But a married man has to think about his earthly responsibilities and how to please his wife. His interests are divided. In the same way, a woman who is no longer married or has never been married can be devoted to the Lord and holy in body and spirit. But a married woman has to think about her earthly responsibilities and how to please her husband. I am saying this for your benefit, not to place restrictions on you. I want you to do whatever will help you serve the Lord best, with as few distractions as possible."
I Corinthians 7:32-35(NLT)

I know there are many hurting single ladies out there who need balance and need healing in order to move forward. Having been married most of my life, since I was nineteen, I cannot speak from experience on the do's and don'ts of singleness. So I asked my daughter Elyzabeth, who is single and a mighty woman of God, and is walking out her singleness as a parent, a woman in ministry, a divorcee and a full time law enforcement employee. When I asked her how does she balance it all, and what wisdom tips would she give to those that need to balance their singleness, she provided seven wise Christian "**Singleness Principles**" to live by:

(1) Make spending daily time with God a priority. He is your husband. Protect and build your intimacy with Him so that you will not be disconnected from The Source, Jesus Christ. There is no substitute for the time you spend with the Lord.

(2) If you are parenting and your children are under 18 years of age, they must have priority over your work in the church or ministry. You can't be involved in everything. Set your limits and boundaries. Make sure you get your children to bed on time, attend their sports and special events. If you have to miss a church event, the choir will still sing on. Remember the church won't say "no." You have to say "no." Don't allow

the church to pimp you and your time.

(3) Single women have to set time for themselves. You will give and give and it is not wise to give out and not replenish yourself. You must to have time to "enjoy life." If you don't take some time out for yourself you will become bitter, and others will begin to take you for granted. Value yourself.

(4) Know your limitations. Some people can kiss or be kissed and they can handle it. Other women can kiss or hold hands and they become overwhelmed with the temptation to "go all the way." Keep yourself out of compromising situations.

(5) Don't be afraid to ask for help. When you are bearing the weight of parenting, provision, protector, and priest of the home, God will give you a support system to help you. Create a support system of those in church, family and friends that can help you balance various tasks. You can't be everywhere and do everything yourself. You will break down and burn out. Just because you ask for help does not mean you are not a good parent or a responsible person in ministry. Get deliverance from your guilt and insecurities.

(6) Many single women that have made mistakes in their marriages and are divorced tend to be paranoid about making another mistake. It is important to get to know the Lord and His Voice the next time around, and be on alert to your personal red flags and his red flags in the relationship. Don't live in fear of remarriage. Thank God for what you have learned and that you are alive. Use precaution but don't be paranoid. Get some deliverance from past hurts and broken relationships with men in your life.

(7) One of the biggest areas of hurt for most single women is from the "spirit of rejection." Rejection by men, rejection by family, rejection by the Church and self-rejection. It's time to work on these areas of rejection because it will affect the way you make decisions for the future. It will also affect the way you parent and the way you serve in ministry.

In my counseling experiences as a Senior Pastor, another area that leads to deep hurt for single Christian women is falling into *lesbian relationships*. Single women must guard against being so needy and emotionally dependent on "other women," that they fall into "lesbian relationships." This is an entrapment of the enemy. Because of hurts by men in your life, (ex-husbands and ex-boyfriends),women make unspoken vows to never be involved with a man again. Lesbian relationships usually evolve out of great emotional needs between two women that start out balanced at first, but then there is a "boundary line" that gets crossed. She begins to desire the "forbidden things" and desire to meet each other's emotional with sexual fulfillment. Guard against UNGODLY SOULTIES WITH WOMEN AND ALSO WITH MEN. There must be "healthy balance and boundaries" in our singleness, as well as in married life.

Also, keep yourself out of compromising situations with married men in the church. Never get closer or more common with "a married man" than his wife is. If you find that you are becoming attracted to and fantasizing about married men or your male Senior Pastor, this is a red flag. It means that there is a need that you are trying to fill illegally. You have crossed a boundary line. Guard against being counseled by the opposite sex especially during vulnerable times in your life. If you must, meet with the pastor and his wife. Always be alert that during those emotional "rollercoaster times" in our lives, the enemy knows you are a little off balance, and he will set a trap for you.

Lastly, one of the areas that I find is prevalent with women in ministry that are single and gifted in so many areas, is that they deal with **loneliness. It is a subtle weapon of the enemy that opens us up to spiritual warfare**. Loneliness can manifest itself in a many ways. Many single women in ministry are "seduced by loneliness." On the other hand, I want to caution married women. **Unfortunately, you can be married and lonely**. Loneliness is defined as being by oneself, solitary, companionless, friendless and forsaken. Just by the definition, you know that loneliness is not of God. For if we are in close relationship with God, He promised never to leave us or forsake us. Loneliness is a demonic spirit that isolates us and brings in multiple other spirits. In my study on the spirit of loneliness, I found that it is like a centipede with one hundred legs hanging around dark and damp places and usually grows at a rapid rate. Loneliness is like the centipede. It can grow and get out of hand. It has many legs.

Also, I want to say here that being in the ministry can also be a lonely place. Those of us who have paid the price to follow Jesus know that it means to be separated out many times and coming out from among those that are familiar to us. Many of the Old Testament prophets experienced times of loneliness for they left family, friends, and some were even forbidden by God to marry (Jeremiah) Still others were persecuted by governmental systems. It was lonely in the earth realm at times walking away from the familiar and walking with God in the supernatural. Many pastor's wives and minister's wives are lonely because they "cannot let their guard down or become common." They are on constant guard and cannot share their true feelings. It's lonely in ministry, but we are never alone. The Lord is with us. We have to learn how to overcome the spirit of loneliness that tries to attach itself to us. Loneliness can tempt us to do things that we would not normally do. Loneliness makes you focus on self more than any other person.

FIRST AID

Reflection: SPIRIT OF LONELINESS

Identify the entry points where the spirit of loneliness is entered your life.

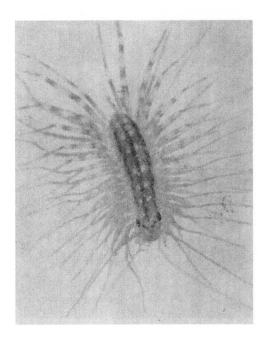

Fear	Rejection	Emotions	Relationships	Spiritual
failure	self hatred	oppression	sexual perversion	pride
torment	pity	depression	attention spirit	neglect
worry	unworthy	hopelessness	misfit	secrecy
anxiety	isolation	grief	cover up	procrastination
lies	separation	draining spirits	divorce	unforgiveness
	wounded spirit	addictions	betrayal	unconfessed sin
	suicide	incubus spirits	false obligations	uncleanliness
	premature death	fantasy	widowhood	double minded
	death wish	vain imaginations	covenant breaker	forbidden desire
		mental illness	comparison	unstable
		compulsive behaviors		

Trauma	Church Hurts	Betrayal	Childhood
infirmity	from pastor/ leadership	parents	traumas
abuse	offense	siblings	hurts
criminal behavior	betrayal	friends	neglect
incarceration	spiritual abuse	church	illness
abandonment		tworkplace	disabilities
		spouse	fatherlessness

When dealing with the spirit of loneliness we must have accountability in our lives on many levels. Accountability keeps us connected to others who can give us wise counsel and bring us into balance. Where there is loneliness that is not dealt with, you will find imbalance in our lives.

Satan loves to isolate us and bring imbalance in our lives. Women of God that are married or single must not allow loneliness to overtake them.

Balanced in Marriage

There is a grace upon our lives to be married to a preacher. We cannot do it in our own strength and flesh. When my husband was installed, so was I. That ceremony of installation was a statement to principalities and powers that God's hand, and God's grace was upon us as a couple, and we were commissioned to a divine assignment. *This grace for marital balance* was evident more and more as we faced trials and tribulations. The enemy had plans to destroy our marriage from the beginning. But we stayed in the will of God and the way of God. That grace upon us kept us from crumbling and being crushed by religious spirits and demonic spirits. Because of our love for God, for each other and the people of God, the enemy could not get a foothold. Love brought balance when nothing else could. Pastoral marriages need this special grace upon them because of the many things their marriage must encounter on behalf of others. Because my husband and I prayed together, we had more balance than most couples in ministry.

We also kept out "third party" interference from in-laws and out-laws. We also kept a certain amount of "simplicity" in our marriage and that kept us somewhat balanced. We worked on our marriage and made time for anniversaries and time away from the pressures of ministry. It was years and years before we were able to take a cruise, but year after year we purposed to celebrate in simple and romantic ways. We never let the church be the "other woman." Yes, there were times it got busy and there were times we felt overwhelmed and absorbed. But we were always able to step back, slow down and remind ourselves that our marriage was birthed before the ministry or parenthood.

Another thing I want to say about marital balance is, it's hard for the wife to be balanced if her husband is imbalanced. The Bible is clear that Jesus Christ is the head, then the husband, then the wife and children. Many pastor's wives and minister's wives have husbands who really love the Lord, but they are out-of-balance. There are several reasons pastoring husbands may be suffering from imbalance:

(1) They can get a "big head." Some pastors get full of pride and the spirit of importance, and you can't tell them anything. You wonder who you really married. Now that they have this new title and authority, there is great imbalance in communication and relationships with wife and children. They become too important for their own good. Anyone with a real "big head" suffers from imbalance and their equilibrium is off.

(2) Many pastors don't have a real consistent prayer life. When our husbands don't have a strong prayer life, there will be imbalance in every area of his life. We can pray for him and the church, but we cannot maintain his relationship with the Lord.

(3) Many pastors lack biblical accountability over them or someone that can hold them accountable and speak truth to them.

(4) Some pastors try to be all things to the church and do not prepare or train others to lead and carry the load. They need to

release and delegate more responsibilities to others, in order to bring balance to his life, family and the church.

(5) Many pastors do not listen to their wives, whom God has really set as a watchman, as a confidant, and in many cases a "seer," one that sees or discerns spiritually and can discern motives of persons. This prophetic gifting in her is not only for his protection, but for the Body of Christ as well.

(6) Some husbands do not see or respect their wives as being on the team with them, a co-laborer, one that has a valuable contribution to make other than sex and household duties. Husbands can get out of touch with the move of the Spirit by being too busy to hear the Lord or hear from their wives.

(7) Husbands that are not spending intimate time with their wives and their families can open themselves up to spiritual and sexual adultery. Intimacy must be protected by both husband and wife. Husbands become imbalanced when they begin to be more intimate with the church or church staff, other women, and the ministry itself instead of their spouse.

(8) It's important to include here that a major area of imbalance in clergy marriages is domestic violence. I will deal with this in more detail in the Prince Charming chapter. But it is important to note that many Christian men in leadership are not balanced because they are batterers. Many times these pastors (men) have problems with anger management, insecurity, domination and control, and unresolved childhood traumas that they take out on their wives and children.

"Perpetrators of domestic violence are everywhere; some even worship in and lead our churches. There are men who praise God and preach Jesus who also beat, control, curse, rape, and terrorize their wives and girlfriends. Perpetrators of domestic violence can change, but few can do so without long term commitment to work on their issues." 9

"Hold him accountable. Remember, perpetrators of domestic violence rarely take responsibility for their destruction. Instead they blame alcohol, children, drugs, job stresses, mood swings, Satan and especially, their victims." 10

When our husbands are balanced, that balance flows down to us and the children. When our husbands are balanced and he is the Senior Pastor, it flows down to the church as well. God expects us to balance our time and all that He has given us stewardship over. After you have prayed for wisdom to balance, then you have to set your priorities and put them into place. We must not allow the adversary to appeal to our fleshly tendencies and tempt us beyond our God given boundaries of grace, revelation, experience and provisions that God has assigned and allotted to each of us.

Balanced in Motherhood

I began to teach on the topic of *Balancing Marriage, Ministry and Motherhood* after I had been married and in ministry about twenty years. Our children were in high school and middle school by that time, and so my reflections in this chapter are truly from personal experience. One of the first things I want to share with you is that I had no prior help or wisdom given to me about balancing marriage, motherhood and ministry. It was truly trial and error. The order of things for me was God first, my husband, my children, the church or ministry and then myself. I think for the most part I had balance, but I would not advise women of God to "neglect themselves." I really neglected myself of necessary things in order to make sure that my husband and children and yes, the church, were taken care of first, and my needs came last or not at all. Today, my physical health would probably be better had I prioritized differently. God never requires of us to neglect ourselves of those necessary or basic things because that's not going to bring Him glory.

God has been good to me because I have lived a sacrificial life and I didn't complain about it. Though it seemed that I had forgotten about myself, God did not forget me. After sacrificing and giving to others to advance them for at least the first fifteen years of my marriage, God spoke to me and said "Daughter, it's your time." God began to open doors for me to fulfill the calling on my life also. This was a progressive shift and I had to war with guilt, and I had to get my mind renewed and prepared for the new season that I was entering. I had to learn that it was alright to take care of myself and pamper myself from time to time. It was alright to spend time allowing the Holy Spirit to perfect me and pamper me.

I have no regrets about being a "stay home mom." My only regret was that it meant poverty for us because the church salary was minimal and we lacked dependable health benefits. Our children did not get to be involved in sports and extra-curricula activities. They were nurtured in the church and sheltered, but my choice to stay home and raise them and live on one income was not easy. I knew my husband and I were rearing up "Levites" or "faithful priests." I could not allow them to be reared by ungodly or careless daycare centers. I wanted to be the one to nurture them, feed them, teach them and prophesy over them. God let me see the callings on their

lives very young. I felt it was necessary for as me a mother to lay
foundation in their lives and that my time would come later to be
launched in ministry. I am sharing this because we must protect our
spiritual legacy. Unfortunately, some churches that we serve in will
not always protect our children. They will use our children, but
will also discard them just as quick. If you must work while your
children are young, you will have to balance your time with them and
deprogram them of ungodly influences. We protected our children
from Halloween and occult influences, as well as the Christmas rush
for toys. Instead we planned family get aways at Christmas without
toys, but lots of family fun, food and time together. The kids say
even today, the non commercial Christmas was so valuable to them.
Remember: we as pastoral families are raising faithful priests unto
the Lord, and it won't be easy. When our children were older and
in middle school and high school, I was able to go back to work. I
never understood how the Proverbs woman in Proverbs 31 did all that
she did. I know now:

**She had to make a decision or prioritize what was most
important in each season of her life. She moved from season
to season with the Word of the Lord directing her. She was
an "amplified woman" not a copy cat.** She had certain virtues
or qualities in her life that gave her balance and caused her to be

tremendously fruitful. A pastor's wife, minister's wife, woman preacher, or godly woman must have certain virtues flowing in her life to walk in balance.

*"Who can find a virtuous and capable (**balanced**) wife? She is more precious than rubies. Her husband can trust her, and she will greatly enrich his life. She brings him good, not harm, all the days of her life."* Proverbs 31:10-12 (NLT)

One of the things we need most among Christian women today as well as among Christian leaders is a "sense of balance." I define balance as *"giving equal time or attention to persons, places, things or tasks that we deem important in that season, so that none of those things are neglected, and we also are the blessed by our efforts, and not burned out by them."* Divine balance is seen in the life of the Proverbs woman. Balance in her life makes her more precious than rubies. **You can't buy balance.** Balance is the blessing of living a real Christian life and walking in the wisdom of God. Balance is what the world should see in every area of our lives because we are filled with the Spirit of God. I often wondered how could the Proverbs 31 woman could do all that she did, or how did Deborah wear so many hats for some forty years and not burn out? I believe Deborah and other women of God are mentioned in the Scriptures to show us that *the greater balance we have, the greater glory we can bring to the Lord!*

Everything in our lives works better when we are balanced. New tires on our car run smoother when balanced. The checkbook must be balanced. We must have a balanced diet every day. Nations, businesses and churches and individuals must balance their budgets. The earth needs balance and because it's out of balance we are experiencing Global Warming. We need balance in relationships, especially the family. We are standing on the Word of God in this generation and the next for marriages to continue to be defined as a "union between a male and female," so the family can be balanced. Every pastor and pastor's wife need to be balanced individuals because of the great demands that will be put upon their lives. Ministry is demanding and without balance, marriage, family and ministry will suffer.

Balanced in Ministry

John the Baptist, the forerunner of Jesus Christ, had a balanced estimation of himself and his ministry. He knew that no matter how people flattered him and tried to promote his ministry, he knew he was only a forerunner. He knew that his ministry would remain balanced as long as he stayed within his calling and stayed in "his lane." So many of us get out of our lane, or our sphere of ministry that God has called us to.

"He confessed, he did not deny, but confessed, "I am not the Christ."

John 1:20 (KJV)

This statement is key to us being balanced in ministry. We must remember that we are not the Savior; we are **not** the Christ; and we are not the answer. Jesus is the answer. Sometimes we get it twisted and we may not say anything about Christ, but we insinuate the ministry stops with us. We have to be careful not to usurp our authority and exalt ourselves as the Redeemer. It's easy to do. How? We take the glory and the credit; we get people depending on us for everything; we get a spirit of importance on us; we forget the people belong to God and not us; we build our own kingdoms instead of the Kingdom of God. Yes, it's easy to get imbalanced when we become self-centered and not Christ-centered in ministry. Balance begins by always acknowledging that Jesus Christ is the Head of the Church and we are His Body.

Ministry is demanding. Do you keep pouring into others while we neglect to be replenished yourself? Imbalance comes upon us when we are drained and tapped out from serving and keep running on empty. We must know our limitations and we must know when we need personal ministry and a refilling of the Holy Spirit.

Jesus is our master example of *balance in ministry*. Balance for Christians always begins on our knees in prayer. You can't have balance without an activated prayer life. There are "Seven P's" I want to suggest for spiritual balance for men and women of God. These principles come from my own personal experiences.

The Seven P's for Spiritual Balance

1. PRAYER LIFE - No prayer life, no balance. Slow down your pace to pray and talk to God. Balance comes upon us in that "secret place." We must listen for His voice and He will let us know when we are out of balance and out of touch. God taught me how to pray and how to listen to His voice first. That was the beginning of walking in spiritual balance. Jesus balanced the demands of ministry because his prayer life kept Him connected to the Father. He ministered to the Father first, and then to the crowds.

"Before daybreak the next morning, Jesus got up and went out to an isolated place to pray." Mark 1:5(NLT)

"But when you pray, go away by yourself, shut the door behind you, and pray to your Father in private. Then your Father, who sees everything, will reward you." Matthew 6:6 (NLT)

(2) PRIORITIZE - Major on the major things in the right season. Jesus had His priorities in order. His priorities were determined by God's will for His life and in the right season. Some things may need to be cancelled or you may have to say "no" to some things in that season. Many pastors, pastor's wives and churches are doing good things, but in the wrong season. You may need to re-distribute the work load and share the work with others. TIME IS PRECIOUS AND CANNOT BE RECYCLED.

(Jesus at the wedding in Cana) "Dear woman, that's not our problem," Jesus replied. My time has not yet come." John 2:4(NLT)

"Seek ye first the Kingdom of God above all else, and live righteously, and he will give you everything you need." Matthew 6:33(NLT)

"To every thing there is a season, a time for every activity under heaven" Ecclesiastes. 3:1(NLT)

So many times I meet men and women of God who are struggling with balance, and a lot of times it's because they want to do a "good thing or fulfill a vision God showed them" but it's the wrong season to do it. You will not experience balance if you don't let some things go. You will be drained if you don't manage your time and resources in each season.

We must beware of the "draining spirit" that comes like a "bat spirit" to suck us dry. Pastors and their wives must guard against this spirit.

You can be drained by:

a. Negative people

b. Gossip and frivolous phone conversation

c. People that are dream and vision thieves

d. Crisis situations with no end in sight

e. Church political games and power struggles

f. Religious spirits (Dealing with those who hate progress and change)

g. Personal and church financial battles

h. Dead beat relationships, especially extended family issues

i. Leeches (those that use us for personal gain but care nothing about the ministry or our personal well being.

j. Time thieves (Those that drain our valuable time and warp our schedules and drain our brain power) Beware.

Satan comes to drain mental strength, thoughts and ideas, life and vitality, dreams and visions, joy and peace, and especially your prayer time with God. The drainer loves to drain your "intimate time" with your spouse and your family.

(3) PREPARATION - Balance requires discipline physically, mentally, academically and spiritually. Last minute preparation only brings frustration and stress. We must consecrate our bodies to the Lord in order to walk in divine balance. Holy living requires preparation to walk in balance. Balance is connected to caring for your body, eating nutritiously, exercise, and getting ample rest and sleep. Spiritual balance requires daily time with the Lord in prayer, Bible reading and study of the Word. Time management is key to walk in daily balance.

> *"Work hard so you can present yourself to God and receive his approval. Be a good worker, one who does not need to be ashamed and who correctly explains the word of truth."*
> *II Timothy 2:15 (NLT)*

(4) PASSION - Passion and pursuit of our purpose and destiny for our lives will keep us balanced. Our passion is our "first love." Balance comes upon our lives when we keep our passion for Christ first, and the fire of the Lord guides us into the things He has called us to. We can be easily tempted and pulled away into other things. Balance is fueled by the passion God had put in your heart. So many of us are doing things that we have no passion for, but we are filling in because there is no one else to do it or we took on more than we could handle to keep the peace. Our God given passion is connected to balancing in our lives.

"But I have this complaint against you. You don't love me or each other as you did at first. Look how far you have fallen. Turn back to

Me and do the works you did at first." Revelation 2:4-5(a) (NLT)

(5) PLEASURE- Fun and play time is part of the fabric of a balanced Christian life. Balance comes from times of refreshing, rest, and relaxation in the Lord and with your family. So many pastors and wives have become dull and boring because they have become so religious and fun and enjoyment has gone right out the window. Their children are spiritual zombies and have become glued to church pews when they should be playing football, soccer and going on family vacations. We must carve out time to get away from church work. If you don't have a church that is able to bless you with vacations and times of leisure, this can be challenging at times, especially on one income. We were not able as a family to travel or take vacations until I went back to work. My income helped to release funds for family time, vacation, and trips for my husband and I.

"Come to me, all of you who are weary and carry heavy burdens, and I will give you rest. Take my yoke upon you. Let me teach you , because I am humble and gentle at heart, and you will find rest for your souls. For my yoke is easy to bear, and the burden I give you is light."Matthew 11:28-30 (NLT)

(6) PRECEPTORS (Mentors) - We all need someone in our lives who has been where we are going. We need to be open,

teachable and willing to make adjustments in order to bring about balance in our lives. We need a Word of wisdom to bring balance in our lives. I thank God for seasoned pastor's wives and women in ministry that helped me by just talking to me and praying for me. I was able to find women of God that could keep confidentialities. We need the wisdom from those who have a proven walk in the God and fruit that remains. We need someone that can tell us how they balance their life and ministry so we don't have to repeat their mistakes. We need to make some minor adjustments. Sometimes just a "word in season" from an experienced pastor's wife or seasoned woman in ministry is all we need to get back in balance.

(7) PRAISE AND WORSHIP – Worship keeps us balanced because it always brings us back to God and restores our souls. Our souls need balance. Our souls really get balanced when we learn how to "be still before the Lord." We need our souls to be washed and mended from all the things that wound the soul. Praise and worship has a way of putting everything back into right perspective. We get our minds off our problems and focus on Jesus, the Problem Solver. When we turn our hearts toward heaven, and the gates of hell cannot prevail. There is something about the true worship of the Lord that brings healing and restores balance to our minds, bodies and souls. In praise and worship we can taste and see that the Lord is good. We are called to bless the Lord at all times. Blessing the Lord brings us back into balance.

Let's look now at signs of imbalance that we must be guarded against.

31 Signs of Imbalance

1. Overwhelmed…you are wearing too many hats

2. You have lost your time of intimacy with the Lord

3. Depression (loss of peace, joy and hope)

4. Complaining and murmuring (never satisfied)

5. Resentment and bitter roots (mean and nasty)

6. Infidelity (Extramarital affairs)

7. Un forgiveness, offense and grudges

8. Spiritually dry, low desire for the Word or spiritual growth

9. Neglecting your spouse and children

10. Misplaced your priorities

11. Juggling finances (robbing Peter to pay Paul)

12. Your spouse and children are complaining about not getting equal time and attention from you

13. Complaints from the church about your imbalance

14. Loss of sensitivity to the Spirit of God (can't hear God)

15. Irritable, tired or fatigued

16. Backsliding

17. Addictions

18. Adultery (Spiritual or Sexual)

19. Turning to occult and witchcraft alternatives to find balance

20. Not eating, sleeping or resting properly

21. Poor time management, time waster, poor preparation

22. Drained and open to infirmity

23. Late, undependable or procrastinating

24. Desire for forbidden things and open to demonization

25. Worry and anxiety

26. Instability or transient behavior/unstable

27. Compulsive Behaviors

28. Lack of self control and spiritual discipline

29. Not able to give love and compassion or receive it

30. Infirmity and sickness (immune system low)

31. Uncontrolled burst of anger and violence and abuse of others

Balance in our lives is a major area of spiritual warfare. We must take time to restore balance by first slowing down and getting still before the Lord. He will speak to our hearts and help us get things in divine order.

GET BACK IN BALANCE ON THE CROSS

Jesus Christ our Lord had perfect balance. He is our example. I see Him hanging on the cross. Nailed to the cross, He hung there because "balance needed to be restored between God the Father and mankind. The cross was the "balance beam" God used to bring us salvation. The cross is vertical and horizontal. Christ had his vertical relationship with God in tact. He died so that the horizontal relationship with mankind would be restored. We see balance in the Lord's life with His priority on His relationship with the Father and human beings. Balance is always vertical and horizontal. When we get out of touch vertically with God and struggle in our relationships horizontally, we are definitely getting out of balance. If we can keep the greatest commandment, we will be in balance with God and our neighbor.

Jesus replied, " 'Love the Lord your God with all your heart and with all your soul and with all your mind.' This is the first and greatest commandment. And the second is like it: 'Love your neighbor as yourself.' All the Law and the Prophets hang on these two commandments."
Matthew 22:37-40 (NIV).

Divine balance requires that we must be men and women of prayer and **intercession**. Intercession brings balance for it reveals to us the true heart of God for us. **Integrity** brings balance. Righteous living sets the standard for balance in every area of our life. **Intimacy** with the Lord through worship and time alone with Him brings forth balance. For in that time of intimacy we are impregnated with the purposes and plans of God and the wisdom and revelation of God. We need ongoing guidance and **instruction** by the Spirit of the Lord to maintain balance. We need to be **intoxicated** with the Spirit of God. To be filled with the Spirit of God is our insurance policy that we will be balanced and filled with the mind of God for in singleness, marriage, motherhood and ministry. We must take **inventory** of what's going on in our lives from time to time to stay balanced. And finally we must **inquire of the Lord** and He will reveal to us areas of imbalance and how to bring balance and glory to Him.

The Rewards of Being Balanced in Ministry

David lived a life of simplicity and solitude out in the fields shepherding the sheep, which is a requirement for spiritual balance. People will know when you are balanced and there will be rewards for living a balanced life.

1. The Spirit of the Lord comes upon us in greater measure.

    I Samuel 16:13

2. God looks for those that are balanced (David) to replace those that are no imbalanced. (Saul) The Spirit of the Lord lifts or departs from those that ruled inadequately or out of balance. When God gets ready to remove imbalanced leaders, He looks for balanced ones to anoint to take their place. *I Samuel 16:14*

3. God will promote those that are balanced. You will be sought out by those who once were in Saul's camp to come and follow you and dwell in your camp with the Lord. Those who had no use for you before will now begin to call upon you. *I Samuel 16:16-17*

4. Favor comes to those that are balanced. People will send for you and you will find favor with those who before would not give you

the time of day. *I Sam 16:19-22*

5. A refreshing and anointing of fresh oil comes to those that are balanced. The balance upon your life will refresh even your enemies and demons will flee because of the anointing upon you.

I Samuel 16:23

6. You can defeat your giants and overcome the enemy when you are balanced. Don't fear your giants. Giants and problems are conquered easily when we are balanced in the Lord. Boldness comes upon you. I Samuel 17:1-9

7. We have greater victory over Satan in times of testing. Your balance will be tested. God will set up a situation for you to be tested. Satan will also test your level of balance by sending situations to throw you off balance. But when you are balanced you can fight the enemy's surprise attacks. No fear or hesitation was found in David.*I Samuel 17:32*

Balance is key for longevity and success in ministry. It is also key for our children. They learn by what we do, not always by what we say. They need to see balance in the parsonage and in our every day lives. Many preacher's kids vow to leave the church due to the imbalances they saw growing up in the parsonage and in the pews. In other words, "lack of balance in marriage, motherhood and ministry is a poor witness for the Lord.

Prayer and Reflection

Journal and pray about the areas you need balance in. Discuss or list the areas you need the Lord to help you bring balance. Date this journal. Watch the Lord work with you and through you in the days, months and years to come.

Chapter 5

The Wounded Lady

(A Vision)

While I was attending a prayer conference in Anaheim, California one year, I was assigned to the prayer room as an intercessor to pray during the conference. There were intercessors there from all over the region and we did not know each other. I entered the room and there were men and women in the room from all ethnic backgrounds and denominations. As I began to join in and pray in the Spirit, the Lord began to move among us. A brother in the Lord walked over to me and said, "*you are one of them*." I looked at him and wondered what he was talking about. I said, "I beg your pardon, what do you mean?" He said, "The Spirit of the Lord spoke to me about you when you entered the room. I know you don't know me, but by the Spirit of the Lord I know you. God said "You are one of His daughters that has been severely wounded for His sake." I began to well up inside and tears began to flow.

Then David, told me about the vision he had. In this vision, three women came before the throne of God. They were all women of prayer who had been laboring for the Kingdom. They all were in white and had their heads and faces veiled with beautiful white silken cloth. As they came to the throne of God, they continued to lay souls before the throne, for they had been out harvesting souls for the Kingdom. But somehow one of the veils over the face of one of the women was unveiled. I saw her deeply scarred face. I cringed and said "Father, what happened to her?" The Father spoke to me and said, "She is one of them. She has been busy doing the work of the Kingdom, but the church has rejected and scarred her deeply. The men in the Body of Christ have used her but also rejected her. She is one of my precious handmaidens that will not be denied her calling and purpose. She continues to bring in souls no matter what. These are the women that have bore great sacrifice for preaching the Gospel, for serving as pastor's wives and minister's wives, for being misunderstood, and yes, even from much domestic abuse. She is *one of them*, my son."

After David finished sharing this vision with me, I wept deeply and he prayed for me. I was no longer ashamed of my wounds and scars, for I knew I was "one of them" that belonged to the Father. I needed to keep on bringing in the harvest and not let anyone or anything deny me the satisfaction of obeying God and being about My Father's business. After this experience with David, without a doubt, I knew that someday, everything would be reconciled. Everything that I had ever suffered would be brought to justice by My King and the real culprit, Satan, would get his eternal sentence in the Lake of Fire.

This chapter is for those wounded ladies that thought the Lord had forgotten them. But because you are "**one of them**," God will never forget you.

My greatest and deepest wounds did not come from the world but from the church, the denomination, vicious women, and the Body of Christ at large. It was the *friendly fire* of: spiritually crippled and controlling church leaders; fearful and jealous women; male chauvinism; and denominational police, that could have destroyed me. There are many casualties among pastors and wives that are now out of the church, out of their minds, and out of their destiny and purpose, due to the wounds. Who ever heard of going to church and being worse off? Well, it is happening all across America in churches today. There are not many pastors and wives who can say they are "wound-free."

I also want to dedicate this chapter to those coming into ministry that have no idea what they are getting into. I had somewhat of a fairy tale image of pastoring, and saw it as a life that would be fulfilling, and that everyone would love and accept you because you are doing the work of God. I had no concept of enemies in the church; nor, did I know the depth of ruthlessness connected to people in authority and the power struggles in the church. Those that are coming into pastoral ministry, especially the wives, must expect to be wounded but not allow the wounds to make you bitter. I can't imagine why seasoned pastor's wives let young pastor's or minister's wives suffer and wander on their own. Pastor's wives should stick together and encourage and nurture one another regardless of the issues that divide us denominationally.

Gayle Haggard, author of A Life Embraced: A Hopeful Guide for the Pastor's Wife, said "ministers' wives can feel isolated because of a misconception about leadership, since they and their husbands are leaders of their congregations. They can feel trapped by unrealistic expectations to live a certain way, to dress a certain way, for their children to behave a certain way… and ministers' wives often find themselves handling more jobs than they expected to take on. You're not really hired, and yet there is some expectation in most church settings that the pastor's wife come along in a package deal," said Becky Hunter, current president of the Global Pastors Wives Network. **11**

I realized that I was alone and that people expected you to "just know what to do and say" when you became the pastor's wife. But I was hungry for someone (a seasoned pastor's wife) to tell it like it is. I began to seek them out and found that many of them didn't reach out because they were dealing with their own wounds and hurts. Then I founded an organization called Endurance Seminars for Pastor's and Minister's Wives. It was the only "intimate" outreach to pastor's and minister's wives in my area that didn't have a status and social club atmosphere. I would invite three seasoned pastor's wives as speakers and they would tell their stories and give wisdom and insight. We then had lunch together and afterwards more afternoon sessions. At the close of each Endurance Seminar, I would present a plaque to these women heroines. Many of them had never received anything for their leadership as women in pastoral ministry with their husbands. This continued for five years and at least 15 pastor's wives were honored and several hundred women were better equipped for the spiritual warfare they faced. New and young women that are ministers and ministers wives need to connect to seasoned women. This is not a profession one can just read about. In order to be a well rounded pastor's wife, minister's wife or woman in ministry, **you need mentoring relationships with other women in ministry to provide accountability; sound counsel; survival techniques; regular retreats; growth opportunities; and ongoing deliverance.** You also need regular times of personal selah and family vacations.

Many preacher's wives are the "walking wounded." They continue to give out and serve bitter waters that spew out of their hearts and sometimes their mouths. They have been so busy serving they have not realized they have been "wounded in the war." As a pastor's wife I do understand what it's like to be a Wounded Lady, and that we need special ministry, not from those that wounded us, but those that can speak truth and life back into us and hold us accountable for our actions.

The Bible is clear in Isaiah 53 that our Lord and Savior Jesus Christ was the most wounded and despised of all men. But He did not allow that to hinder His mission. I believe we can learn some things from His life and from the lives of those who have gone before us. Isaiah gives us a clear picture of the life and ministry of Christ. It was not pretty, yet because of His wounds many were healed. We will be wounded, but we must make sure that many are healed because of our wounds. That is why I write as many books as I can to bring healing for the wounds I have endured. I want to reach as many believers as possible and especially the wounded handmaidens of the Lord, to bring healing and hope because of the things I have suffered.

ISAIAH 53

1 Who would believe what we have heard? To whom has the arm of the LORD been revealed?

2 He grew up like a sapling before him, like a shoot from the parched earth; There was in him no stately bearing to make us look at him, nor appearance that would attract us to him.

3 He was spurned and avoided by men, a man of suffering, accustomed to infirmity, One of those from whom men hide their faces, spurned, and we held him in no esteem.

4 Yet it was our infirmities that he bore, our sufferings that he endured, While we thought of him as stricken, as one smitten by God and afflicted.

5 But he was pierced for our offenses, crushed for our sins, Upon him was the chastisement that makes us whole, by his stripes we were healed.

6 We had all gone astray like sheep, each following his own way; But the LORD laid upon him the guilt of us all.

7 Though he was harshly treated, he submitted and opened not his mouth; Like a lamb led to the slaughter or a sheep before the shearers, he was silent and opened not his mouth.

8 Oppressed and condemned, he was taken away, and who would have thought any more of his destiny? When he was cut off from the land of the living, and smitten for the sin of his people,

9 A grave was assigned him among the wicked and a burial place with evildoers, though he had done no wrong nor spoken any falsehood.

10 (But the LORD was pleased to crush him in infirmity.) If he gives his life as an offering for sin, he shall see his descendants in a long life, and the will of the LORD shall be accomplished through him.

11 Because of his affliction he shall see the light in fullness of days; Through his suffering, my servant shall justify many, and their guilt he shall bear.

12 Therefore I will give him his portion among the great, and he shall divide the spoils with the mighty, Because he surrendered himself to death and was counted among the wicked; And he shall take away the sins of many, and win pardon for their offenses. (NAB)

We learn from the life of our Lord that we will be wounded many times but those wounds are not for us to fall into pity, but those wounds are our trophies and the foundation that is being laid to help others. Wounds will come with the job description. It is foolish to think you can serve in ministry in any capacity for long and not be hit by a scud missile or two. Ministry is risky. Ask yourself these questions to determine where you are as a risk taker. You may need to take a "reality check."

Are you willing to take the risks of having your heart broken?

Are you willing to live in seasons of great need or poverty?

Are you ready for your children to become targets of angry parishioners?

Is your marriage strong enough to come under scrutiny and attack?

Are you secure in our marriage enough to withstand attacks from Jezebel?

Are you ready to freely give knowing that church folk might not even want to say "thank you" for the sacrifices you have made?

Are you ready for your home to be Grand Central Station, available 24-7, and be a non-stop place of hospitality?

Are you mature enough to get wounded and look beyond the sniper hits but still feed the people and minister in excellence anyhow?

Jesus understands what we are going through. He will heal us again and again. *We learn from the Master that we must forgive those that hurt us. This is hard, but it is the secret to freedom from bitterness and the prison of unforgiveness.* Love overcomes wounds and we must learn to be quick to forgive those that hurt us, or hurt our children and especially those that hurt our husbands. Satan will use "open and bleeding wounds" to disqualify us from our mission. He knows that we cannot minister effectively while wounded and in a place of deep hurt and unforgiveness. Don't let your wounds disqualify you or be the reason you can't fulfill your assignment. Satan loves to see wounded pastors and wives, ministers and leaders, leave the mission field or the ministry, because they couldn't get over past hurts and wounds.

Thank God our wounds can become our testimony and the "stuff that glory is made of." Without trials and tribulations, wounds and war, we have no testimony, and we can't see what glory looks like. Glory is made of human crisis touched by the loving Hand of God. When God is done and brings us through, that human crisis loses it's power over us, and God gets the Glory! Glory is when your suffering is overcome with a powerful testimony of how you made it over. **But we have to be willing to go through the "fire" to get to the glory!** I don't want to get to heaven and meet Apostle Paul, Moses, Deborah,

or Queen Esther and other great men and women of God, and I have
no scars or wounds to show for the sake of Christ. When we get to
heaven, we ought to have some scars and wounds to show the other
great men and women of faith that we have suffered and have scars
to prove it. So many pastors and their wives try to hide their hurts
and wounds. They have made newcomers to the ministry think it is a
bed of roses. We need to repent for "falsifying the ministry." I want
those young couples to know what they are getting into, and that
God has the power to keep them! The pastorate is not for cowards!
The ministry of Jesus Christ is not for cowards and gold diggers! The
ministry of Jesus Christ is not for celebrity saints! It's for the humble,
the faithful worker and for the holy!

Our wounds are evidence and they are our testimony of suffering
for the sake of Christ. When our wounds are healed, then they
become our testimony and trophies. Wounds are necessary to teach
us how to love and bless those that hurt us. Our Lord forgave and
prayed for those that pierced him on the Cross. We must change the
way we have trained our preachers and we must no longer "falsify the
ministry." We must raise up a new breed of leaders that will be able
to contend with the spiritual warfare and not leave the battlefield
with post traumatic ministerial stress. (PTMS)

What is a Wounded Spirit?

A wounded spirit means an injury has taken place in the area of our soul or spirit faculties - mind, emotions and will. It is injury to the unseen areas of our being. The only way others can see the injury is how we behave and conduct ourselves. The deeper or more severe the wounds the greater the negative effect on an individual's life - spiritually, socially, materially and physically, if not dealt with.

The human spirit can endure a sick body, but who can bear a crushed spirit?" Proverbs 18:14 (NLT)

"A cheerful heart is good medicine, but a broken spirit saps a person's strength." Proverbs 17:2 (NLT)

Wounds can be caused by:

- Past or present storms of life that are unpleasant experiences that befall us out of no fault of our own. They include experiences of living under constant negative and critical words; experiences of betrayal (by a loved one; trusted person, or leader); death of a loved one; severe physical or emotional abuse experiences; living under a heavy control and disciplinary environment that brings fear; living under rejection.

■ False accusations; terrible divorce experience (as the victim); traumatic experience(s), severe accident (e.g. surviving the September 11 terror experience, traumatic accident, casualty of war); having a physical or social disability; having a certain physical appearance society "persecutes;" severe racial, gender and ethnic discrimination or abuse; falling victim to false teachings; genuine trials of faith; and so on.

WHAT ARE THE SIDE EFFECTS OF A WOUNDED OR CRUSHED SPIRIT?

Signs that you need to deal with your wounded spirit:

- Nervousness
- Depression and oppression
- Anger, rage, murder
- Defensiveness, very touchy and easily offended
- Extremely self-centered and selfish
- Sleeplessness, insomnia
- Fear, panic attacks
- Escapism, flight, exceptionally withdrawn, loneliness, isolation
- Insecurity, overwhelming guilt and condemnation
- Judgmental, very critical of others, faultfinding
- Unforgiveness, grudges, resentment, vindictiveness, stubbornness
- Lack of concentration, exaggerating the negatives
- Shallow friendships and not able to keep relationships long term
- Blame others
- Self-contempt, self-condemnation, self-hatred
- Addictions, self-destructive behavior, compulsive behaviors

You are being healed of the wounded spirit when you can:

- Pray for those that hurt you
- Love and respect your enemies
- Do good to those that wounded you
- Learn a life long lesson from that pain
- Talk about it and testify and strengthen others
- See your wound as a trophy, not a stumbling block. You have overcome it.
- Have power over it or them, and you can be in the same room with your offender and not be affected by them or your past

Major demonic spirits that must be cast out:

- **bitterness, bitter gall, wormwood**
- unforgiveness, resentment, score keeper
- hatred, self-hatred, murder, rage, anger
- revenge, retaliation
- pain, torment, migraines, mental pain, affliction
- deep hurt, hidden resentment, hidden hurt
- guilt, grief, heartache, unworthy, shame, embarrassment
- betrayal, deception, covenant breaking, Judas, abandonment, lie, falseness, cover up, broken heart
- rejection, fear, condemnation, wandering, pride

Once you identify you have a wounded spirit, it is important to begin to take steps to deal with it so that you will not poison yourself and others. God needs you healed and whole and so does your husband, children, and the people of God. Some pastor's wives have not been diagnosed with clinical depression, but many of them are suffering from it. Seek medical help and advice if your depression is uncontrollable and you even feel like you will harm yourself and others.

Reflection and Prayer

- Don't Repress it- You are the walking wounded. Do not pretend it didn't happen. Holding on to the wound is unhealthy and unwise. Don't hide it. Identify the wound and face it.

- Don't Rehearse it- Do not go over and over it in your mind and torture yourself. Don't dwell on the past. Press toward the future. Do not give it power over you by talking and dwelling on it. Bind up constant memory recall that can drain you. Talking about a thing over and over gives life to it. Watch your words.

- Don't Resent it or those that hurt you- Resentment eats you up. It is called unforgiveness and bitter root. Resentment is like a cancer.
  Get some deliverance.

- Don't Repeat it- Let there be wise gain from your pain. Don't fall into that trap again and again. Learn from this experience. Don't poison others by repeating it over and over.

Make your confession here:

I need to repent of:

I am showing signs of woundedness such as:

I need to receive God's deliverance in the following areas:

Chapter 6

Spiritual Warfare 101

The late Bill Bright, founder of Campus Crusade for Christ
and the Global Pastors Network, gleaned these figures from various
sources a few years ago:

- *Eighty percent of pastors and 84 percent of their spouses feel
  unqualified and discouraged in their roles.*

- *Eighty percent of pastors' spouses feel their spouse is overworked.*

- *Almost 40 percent of pastors polled said they have had an
  extramarital affair since beginning their ministry.*

- *Fifty percent of pastors' marriages will end in divorce.*

- *Eighty percent of pastors' wives feel left out and unappreciated by
  the church members. 12*

There is evidence and statistics to merit the importance of this
spiritual warfare manual. The odds are high for failure of pastoral
families. So many enter this sacred profession unaware of the pitfalls
and pressures. Some never experience the joy of the ministry. The
Word of God gives us our spiritual positioning.

"I am delivered from this present evil world..." Galatians 1:4

"I am seated with Christ in heavenly places..." Ephesians 2:6

"I reside in the Kingdom of God's dear Son..." Colossians 1:13

"Greater is He that's in me than he that is in the world...I John 4:4

"Jesus has made me wisdom, righteousness, sanctification and

redemption..." I Corinthians 1:30

"I can do all things through Christ who strengthens me." Philippians 4:13

Your very spiritual position as a pastor, pastor's wife, or minister of the Gospel, qualifies you to be on the frontline of enemy fire. Woe to the unprepared. The powers of darkness are steadily preparing a showdown to determine your level of spiritual warfare skills. If you are not equipped, you and your family could become a casualty of war. There are too many pastoral leaders who have no "rank in the Spirit." The Devil is not moved by titles. **Only those that can execute the weapons of warfare and move in Christ' spiritual authority can defeat the Devil and forces of darkness.**

I was clueless as a young and new pastor's wife to the dimensions of spiritual warfare that my husband and I were about to encounter in our first church. We loved God, but were not really prepared to take on the territorial, religious and witchcraft warfare of the region. We only had a small glimpse of warfare from the pews and basically none that took place in the parsonage. While in seminary we were in the midst of many clergy couples who were weathering their personal storms behind closed doors. Very few couples shared their fears or struggles openly. After all, if you were a pastor or pastor's wife, you had to put forth an image that "you had it all together." No one told us that 80% of pastors and 84% of pastor's wives feel unqualified and discouraged in their role as a pastoral family. Why didn't someone tell us in seminary that 80% of seminary and Bible college graduates who enter into the ministry will leave the ministry within five years? No one prepared us for the fact that 80% of pastor's wives wish their husbands were in another profession and that he would be overworked and underpaid. Why didn't someone prepare us to deal with depression and discouragement? Whose suppose to teach pastors and pastors wives or women in ministry that demons do exist and that witchcraft is real?

I am convinced and convicted that we must prepare and train our ministers of the Gospel much differently than we were trained. We have to change the devastating and failing statistics. Every clergy couple or woman in ministry needs to be equipped in the area of spiritual warfare and be able to exercise wisdom as well as discernment of spirits.

I define spiritual warfare as:

"An *advanced method of praying* by which we *bind* demonic powers and *loose* the power of God over persons, organizations, neighborhoods, regions or nations, so that those who have been blinded to the truth of the Gospel will able to receive Jesus Christ as Lord and Savior. Spiritual warfare prayer is a *frontal assault* to the kingdom of darkness in the name and authority of Jesus Christ. Spiritual warfare prayer is not for babes in Christ, but *for mature believers* that understand the power of the Blood, the Word and the Name of Christ and are willing to *pray the price* for the Kingdom of God to come in their church, city, region or nation. Spiritual warfare is a military (strategic prayer) operation. It is warfare with invisible forces, against an ancient foe, the Devil and his cohorts, who are very skilled in their craft." **13**

I got introduced to spiritual warfare in our first church. There was an elderly church mother who would come by and sit and chat with me at the parsonage and she basically was the welcoming committee. She would tell me the church history and she began to reveal the history that was not-so-holy and exposed those things that went on behind the scenes. She talked about root working and potions and witchcraft in the church. She made it clear that certain families had strong ties and strongholds on the church. She shared how historically the church was not able to keep a consistent pastor and she believed it was the workings of witchcraft. I remember asking the Lord "why is this woman coming to me?" God said, " *Listen and learn. I will teach your hands to war and your fingers to fight. Daughter, this is the real world of pastoring not only the people, but subduing the powers of darkness.*"

From that time, I gathered and studied the history of the church and the city. I became an avid historian and spiritual mapper. God began to bring revelation and understanding that helped us penetrate the strongholds of the church and region to usher in church growth and prepare the ground for the Gospel. There were many "showdowns" with controlling families and demonic forces as we were breaking strongholds in a one hundred year old church. It took years in the school of prayer with the Holy Spirit to learn to how to war for our children, the church, the city and the region. It was in those early morning times of prayer, where sometimes it was just me and the Lord, that He taught me how to pray, how to trust, how to prophetically see how the enemy had kept this church and region captive. He taught me how to train others. I had become a threat to the kingdom of darkness. No pastoral family had been able to stay at the church for more than a few years. By the grace of God and because we were able to engage in spiritual warfare, our family served that congregation for over twenty years. From that twenty years of on-hands spiritual warfare, I have summarized what I feel are the thirteen dimensions of spiritual warfare that we must be trained in as pastoral leaders, pastors, and ministers' wives, and men and women in ministry. Even our children (PK's) and youth must be trained in spiritual warfare.

13 Dimensions of Spiritual Warfare [14]

1. **Mental Warfare** - A flood of vile thoughts, mental oppression, fear and doubt, forgetfulness, migraines, demonic suggestions and confusion is sent to your mind. The voices of the enemy are strong and speaking continually to weaken the mind.

2. **Physical Warfare** - Unexpected attacks on the physical body, sickness, cancer, infirmities, fatigue, bruises, boils, and all kinds of strange physical attacks. The enemy doesn't want us to learn how to rest, enjoy life, have fun and still be warriors. The enemy seeks to keep us *overwhelmed, unbalanced and in a false transition.*

3. **Communication Warfare** - Demons attack us in our communication lines so we are not able to get instructions or communicate with one another. Spirits of interference and blockage

are sent to keep up confusion and break unity. The spirit of offence is sent to us so that our actions or words are misunderstood and distorted toward one another. The enemy wants us confused, displaced, disconnected, and discouraged.

4. **Relationship Warfare**– All of our relationships will come under attack releasing conflicts, betrayals, backbiting, turning on the ministry and one another, family problems and marital problems. Persecution and excommunication from other churches and friends is not unusual.

5. **Financial Warfare**– Leaders and intercessors will be attacked in finances, job security, bank accounts, discrepancies with old bills or litigations arise from the past, garnishment of wages, stress on the church finances, and unexpected expenses that eat away at monies. The enemy will attack your faithful tithers and givers to cause them to leave the church or be attacked in their income. (Spirit of Python is sent to squeeze finances and resources to death)

6. **Emotional Warfare**– This warfare attacks the emotions and causes depression, oppression, mental illness and insanity. The enemy brings up the past and strong condemnation. There are times of crying for no reason and even thoughts of suicide, death and failure.

An emotional rollercoaster is released. The dream realm and ability to concentrate is attacked.

7. **Temptation Warfare**– The enemy will attack in every "weak area" of our lives and tempt us to give up and go back to a lifestyle of sin and slavery. Pressure comes upon us to make you feel unworthy or beyond restoration; or even feel like you cannot escape the enemy's traps. You may even experience new levels of temptation and seduction traps by the enemy.

8. **Religious Warfare**-Religious spirits strongly attack the leadership and intercessors that have come out of tradition and religion. These spirits put pressure on them to go back into the familiar traditions and try to convince them that they are in the minority. They are bombarded with "what people think" about their ministry and the accuser of the brethren spirits work together with religious spirits trying to regain control. Religious spirits try to convince us to obey man and traditions, and deny the power of God.

9. **Indirect Warfare**- We will not be attacked directly all the time, but the attacks will come to our family members near and far. These attacks are meant for the us, but instead targets our spouses, children, co-workers or anyone connected to us that means a lot to

us. This is called indirect assaults.

10. **Sexual Warfare**– Seduction (sex traps) and enticement is sent to seduce single or married persons. Perversion is sent to defile team members. Incubus and succubus spirits (demons) attacks you in your sleep with sexual assaults to overtake you. Sexual enticements and scandal are released also upon leadership, especially pastors and wives and ministers, to discredit their witness and the Gospel.

11. **Witchcraft/Occult Warfare**– Curses and attacks will be sent to the praying churches and spiritual warriors that are really making an impact. The kingdom of darkness will attack anyone that is taking souls from Satan. Word curses, sorcery, divination and psychic prayers come against the ministry or church. False witnesses and slander will be increased to discredit the work of the apostolic and prophetic, and deliverance and healing, which combats witchcraft and the occult.

12. **Territorial Warfare**– The leadership and ministry/church will be attacked by the ruler spirits over the city and region. They will have to contend with hostile forces from the second heaven realm (prince of the power of the air), and they will experience extra warfare from the regional principalities and powers whom they are affecting

and pulling down. Drastic changes in weather, environmental changes, natural disasters, accidents and such can be caused by these master spirits.

13. **Spiritual Development Warfare**-This warfare is released against us to keep us from studying the Word, worshipping, fasting and praying, carrying out our responsibilities, and being on fire for the Lord! The enemy will throwing fiery darts constantly to keep the us from being spiritually alert, and spiritually powerful to carry out our God given commission from the Lord. We must not take shortcuts in your spiritual development or fall into excuses.

Twenty-Five Biblical Ways to Take Authority Over the Enemy in Spiritual Warfare

- Establish your home as a house that serves the Lord - Joshua 24:15
- Know your weapons are mighty not fleshy- II Corinthians 10:4-5
- Use God's power to tread over serpents – Luke 10:19
- Binding and loosing in prayer-Matthew 16:19
- Overcame Satan by the Blood and Word of your testimony–
  Rev. 12:11
- Be seated in heavenly places (a Kingdom view) -Ephesians 2:6
- Let none of these things(hindrances) move you but be determined-

Acts 20:24

- Be more than a conqueror (more than a survivor but a thriver)

  Romans 8:37

- Put on the whole armor of God– Ephesians 6:10-18

- Remembers: as a man thinks in his heart, so he is.– Proverbs 23:7

- Never give up or give in—Proverbs 24:16

- Bless the Lord at all times– Psalms 34:1

- Wait upon the Lord and you shall renew your strength–

  Isaiah 40:31

- Lift up your eyes to the hills (always looking up in every situation)–

  Psalms 121:1

- Remember: death and life are in the power of the tongue–

  Proverbs 18:21

- Remember: All things work together for good to those that love

God and are called according to His purpose - Romans 8:38-39

- Renew your mind daily-Romans 12:2

- Seek the wisdom of God-Proverbs 3:5

- Ask for angelic assistance– Psalms 91

- Guard your heart against bitterness, resentment and unforgiveness–

  Psalms 51:10

- Remember your victory is in the Spirit of the Lord— Zechariah 4:6

- Little by little you will gain greater authority and territory—

  Deut. 7:22

- Don't be anxious or start worrying- Philippians 4:6 and Matthew 6:28-33
- Prophesy to those dry situations - Ezekiel 37
- Do not panic or fear no matter what situation you face - II Timothy 1:7

What Can Make Us Vulnerable to Spiritual Attacks?

In order to keep unnecessary spiritual warfare attacks from coming upon you, make sure you close the gaps and that you are in:

1. Right relationship with God
2. Right relationship with Self
3. Right relationship with Spouse/family
4. Right relationship with Pastoral and spiritual covering
5. Right relationship with Church family/ relationships
6. Right relationship with other believers/larger Body of Christ
7. Right relationship with non-believers/marketplace/world

Once these areas are in rightful order, it is important that you protect yourself when going into battle. There are some hits you don't have to take if you know and obey what God requires.

Here are some of the sins and transgressions, if committed,

especially with any type of frequency or intensity, it can you get you into major trouble with the Lord where He might choose to allow the hedge to be lowered over your life. The lowering of the hedge gives Satan or demons permission to attack us and our families directly. We open ourselves up to attacks when we dabble or get involved in:

1. Rebellion, stubbornness and disobedience toward God and His Word (which is as witchcraft)

2. The occult and secret societies

3. False religions or cults

4. Any part of the New Age Movement

5. The homosexual lifestyle

6. Any type of Satan worshipping group

7. Any involvement with abortion or the abortion industry

8. Abusing alcohol

9. Doing any type of drugs

10. Any type of extreme verbal and/or physical abuse

11. Any type of promiscuous sexual lifestyle

12. Any type of criminal activity

13. Murder and violence

14. Bringing a cursed object into your home

15. Unconfessed generational sins

16. Violations by others toward you that are demonized (rapist, abuser, incest etc.,)

17. Going into an area of warfare that God has not sent you
because you are curious.

Like anything else that requires training and maturity, so does operating in spiritual warfare. There are levels of growth and accountability. Begin with your own personal life first and be able to overcome your personal warfare on a daily basis. You will never be successful or convince the Devil of your spiritual authority if you are still bound in your own personal life.

Without Spiritual Warfare 101 training:

• It will difficult to experience success in marriage and ministry

• Relationships will suffer and unity will be hard to achieve

• The enemy will continue to kill, steal and destroy until we learn how to fast and pray and pull down strongholds

• Witchcraft and lawlessness will increase in the land

• Missionaries sent out to the mission field will be overtaken by witchcraft, divination, mental illness, curses, and death

• We will not be able to subdue the enemy in our own cities and region

• Spiritual blindness cannot be broken in your region

• You will struggle to preach. teach and worship in strong demonic areas where the enemy has claimed it for evil

• There will be major warfare in our marriages, family and ministry and even greater divorce and family dysfunction

- Pastors will be seduced into sexual sin, depression and leaving the ministry
- Church growth and church health will be unfruitful
- Preacher's children and our godly seed will not walk in the fullness of their calling and destiny
- We will not be able to stand against the tricks of the Devil, to defeat and overcome him
- The Body of Christ will be feeble in power and their ability to fulfill the Great Commission
- We will continue to fight one another instead of unseen forces
- We will not learn how to war with our hands and fight with our fingers
- Deception, delusion and discouragement will increase
- The ministry of healing and deliverance will suffer

12 PRECAUTIONS FOR THOSE ENGAGING IN SPRITUAL WARFARE [15]

1. Be submitted to a pastor/spiritual authority and local church as your spiritual covering.

2. Be sure God has called you into that "sphere" of warfare.

3. Enlist the prayer covering of other intercessors to pray for you and your family.

4. Put on the whole armor of God and cover yourself daily by having time with the Lord for personal prayer and personal repentance.

5. Initiate regular times of fasting and prayer to keep yourself spiritually alert and on the cutting edge of what the Holy Spirit is doing.

6. Identify as quickly as possible areas of sin in your life and confess them before the Lord and close all openings for the enemy to attack you.

7. Worship the Lord in Spirit and in truth and bask in His presence on a daily basis. You will find angelic help being released in the presence of the Lord. Don't hesitate to ask God to release angelic help.

8. Don't be a "lone ranger." Don't be out doing your own thing alone. It is wise and good to minister in teams and not in "solo ministry."

9. Make sure you master other basic levels of prayer first: personal level, family warfare, church warfare and then move to city and regional, national and global warfare which is territorial.

10. Know when you are released from a prayer assignment. It is important to discern the seasons of warfare and when it's time to rest.

11. Take care of your physical body and follow a balanced diet and proper rest. Warfare is hard work and affects us mentally, physically and spiritually.

12. Anoint your home and workplace and Church regularly and cleanse from it from contamination and demonic spirits. Make sure you have set your family altar in the places the Lord has instructed you. (home, church, personal office etc.,)

Reflection and Prayer

List your areas of concern under the various levels of warfare you are experiencing.

Seven Levels of Spiritual Warfare

1. Personal Level Warfare-

2. Family Level Warfare-

3. Church Level Warfare-

4. City Level Warfare-

5. Regional Level Warfare-

6. National Level Warfare-

7. Global Level Warfare-

Chapter 7

Pressure in the Parsonage

"We are pressed on every side by troubles, but we are not crushed. We are

perplexed, but not driven to despair.

II Corinthians 4:8 (NLT)

It is interesting that the word parsonage means "an official residence provided by the church for it's rector or pastor and family." **The parsonage should be a place of peace, privacy and purposed for** ministry. For many pastoral families, the parsonage experience is more of a battle ground than a safe haven. Many pastor's wives live right next door to the church or even attached to the same building of the church. It was really not too private for it gave the members constant access to their private lives making it be known as a "fishbowl." It was convenient for the church members, but a living hell for the pastor's wife and children. What was really meant for good, many times brought pressures and not peace to the "First

Family."

Thank God, today many churches have a greater respect for the life of the First Family and dare not put them next door to the church. They are provided with beautiful homes with the needs of the children in mind, and it is usually in a secluded place of beauty and rest in the best areas of town. However, the First Family is still expected to entertain and usually provide hospitality for guest and church functions.

Some of the greatest church hurts for Pastor's wives is the warfare attached to the parsonage. Spirits of control, threatenings, poverty, power struggles, red tape, insecurity, scrutiny, embarrassment, eviction after the death of her husband, lack of intimacy and even witchcraft or root workings plague the parsonage. Churches, trustees and deacons have not always been good stewards of their pastoral families. The pastor's wife can internalize a lot of these ungodly dealings as power plays and not spiritual oversight. Many pastor's wives have "horror stories" about how their families were mistreated at the hand of church authorities.

On the other hand, more and more pastoral families are being treated better and given the respect due them for housing and benefits. Many churches are actually buying a home for their pastoral families and giving them a home as a gift, especially after they have served the church all of their lives. It becomes part of a retirement packet and is a wonderful way to say "thank you" to the servants of God for twenty, thirty and forty years of faithful and sacrificial service to a congregation.

I want to note here that there is always a spiritual battle going on over the parsonage. The reason is that it represents the place of peace, rest and intimacy for the shepherd and his family. When there is not enough money, there are constant worries over making ends meet, poverty and lack, church business meeting debates over the parsonage upkeep and upgrading, tension between the pastor and wife, and the children lacking what they need, this makes for a battleground at the parsonage. Many times the church takes their time making repairs and doing what is needed to make the parsonage a safe and comfortable place.

Worst case scenerio, many pastor's wives have been evicted and put out of the parsonage after the death of the pastor or if the pastor becomes ill and can no longer pastor. The wounds are deep in her heart when she finds out that she had no value other than through her husband. She leaves wounded, abandoned and destitute many times. Many times she leaves wounded, abandoned and destitute. She feels raped and robbed by the church.

This chapter is a call to church leaders to make sure their pastoral family is properly cared for. It leaves many unsettled wounds in the heart of the pastor's wife when injustices are done with the parsonage as the target. Many pastor's wives need healing and deliverance over "nightmares in the parsonage" experiences. Further, the PK's (preacher's kids) are very wounded when there has been church abuse toward their parents. Many pastors and wives are able to buy their own homes and this has eliminated church red tape and horror stories.

FIRST AID

REFLECTION AND PRAYER

Take time in this chapter to begin to lay your heart before the Lord and release those that wronged you and your family in the parsonage. Forgive and release those that hurt you. Let God vindicate you. Trust that the Lord will give you "justice." For He is the great "pay master." List the persons you need to forgive and release as it relates to the care of the parsonage, salaries, benefits, retirement and other areas that relate to the pastoral package. Your husband may need prayer in this area also.

Chapter 8

Domestic Violence in the Parsonage:
A Letter from the Lord

"Dear Daughter,

I am so pleased with you. You are married to one of my sons who is pastoring My flock. I will hold him accountable for you also, as one who is in the flock. No one knows, but I know, what is going on in the parsonage behind closed doors. You have been covering up your bruises well. Even the inner hurts and pains, you can put on a smile and no one knows the abuse. But I know daughter. I see and I have heard your cries. I am not pleased that my son, your pastor, is not loving and giving himself for you like My Son loved and gave Himself for the Church. I am not pleased that you are being mistreated verbally, physically, emotionally and financially. I know you want to keep hiding it and you think that being a good wife means "suck it up" and keep on going. But that is not My will for you daughter.

I have heard your thoughts daughter. You think because you are the Pastor's wife you must bear this burden and a good wife does not want to uncover her husband. A good pastor's wife does not want to be a stumbling block to the work of God. You don't want your husband to be exposed and loose his job and destroy his reputation. You fear that that no one would believe that this mighty man of God, filled with the Spirit is beating his wife. Who do you tell? You don't want to be a victim of divorce and your children suffer from not having a daddy. But you are so afraid that this thing could turn on you, and he might make people think you are the villain and that you are unfaithful or an unfit mother. You are fearful that people will think you are the crazy one and that you are making up lies about his violent behavior. He is such a good actor and a good preacher. He fooled you also for a long time. You have no way of making a living apart from him should things go sour. What are you to do? You keep saying and thinking and praying that he will change but he never does. You keep praying that things will get better or that this problem will go away if you are just a better wife or if you do more and more. But I tell you, the demons of abuse will never be satisfied with anything you do. *Stop thinking you deserve this kind of abuse.*

Well, I will tell you daughter. I love you and I did not call you to be punching bag. My son, your pastor, the preacher, is sick and he is also breaking the law. Daughter, he is an abuser because somewhere he saw others being abused in his midst. He thinks he has a right to abuse you because you are his wife. But that is all contrary to scripture. He is wrong and you must arise daughter and get to a "safe place." You and the children must flee to a safe place and demand that he get help. I will make sure that "some one will believe you daughter" and you will get the help you need.

I will protect you My daughter and the children, but you must begin to deal with the abuse in the parsonage. Do not partner with THE LIE. It is a lie that you are trying to cover up. I am going to allow it to be exposed if the pastor refuses to get help and repent. I shall expose it and I shall cleanse the house of that abusive and lying spirit. *For domestic violence is a sin, and it is a crime and it is a learned behavior.*

So, go my daughter and do the right thing. Truth is always the right thing. And I shall cover thee and protect thee and reposition thee says God. Don't worry about the church, for they are supposed to be a "safe place for thee." But if the church cannot discern his true nature, they cannot help thee, for they are blind and I will hold the church accountable for their neglect. But many daughters are crying like you are to be set free from abusers. Many of my sons cannot preach on abuse because they are the abusers. The church must arise and become a healing place. The church must require disciplinary actions on him.

And my daughter, when this thing is exposed and you are free, I am going to use you to set other women free and help other pastor's wives break the cycle of violence. Be bold and know that I never meant for you to live this way, says the Spirit of the Living God. I have heard your prayers, but now is not the time to pray, it is the time to "act" and make a decision for your safety and the safety of your children. For if you continue in the lie, your sons will also be abusers and your daughters will follow in your footsteps. You must act and you must trust Me says God.

Let go of your pride, let go of your fear, let go of what people will think and most of all let go of this evil soul tie, for it is not of Me, says the Spirit of the Lord. For I am here to set you both free and to use you both if you will walk in truth. I am the Lord, and I am the One that has come to give thee justice, and life more abundantly," says the Lord.

© Copyright 2008, by Bishop Dr. Jackie L. Green, JGM-National PrayerLife Institute, Phoenix, AZ

What is domestic violence?

Domestic Violence is a pattern of power and control over another person through fear and intimidation, and often includes the threat of violence and death. Battering happens when one person believes they are entitled to control another person. Assault, battering and domestic violence are a sin, a crime, and learned behavior.

Are you a Silent Victim?

There are many pastor's wives, minister's wives and women in ministry that are victims of domestic violence or other forms of neglect, and they have been silenced by religion, tradition and false obligations. Their children are also held captive to a code of silence.

What are we going to do about male pastors that are abusers? Where are they going to get help and when are we going to make sure they are accountable and disciplined by the Church?

This chapter is close to the heart of God. He surely loves His daughters and is mindful of how they are treated by His sons. I know there are many women and girls in our churches that are victims of domestic violence and molestation. It is a hidden from view, but not really. If we pay attention to the women in our churches we will see the signs of abuse all around us.

I shall never forget when I was in the grocery store one day. I greeted and hugged a pastor's wife and she seemed cordial but was very withdrawn. She looked worn and unkept, mentally tired, and not so radiant as I remembered her. She was a really beautiful woman, but you could see the erosion and that she had been stripped emotionally and physically of that self esteem and confidence over time. Her conversation was short but I couldn't get one thing out of my mind; *the fear in her eyes*. I often wondered about her and how she was doing, but I didn't want to pry. Her eyes told me everything

I needed to know. I knew she would not share what was going on but I began to pray for her. Even when I wanted to talk or visit with her, I could never get to her for she was under heavy surveillance. She could never come to the phone, or she was always sleep or she might call me back. I knew he was a highly functional alcoholic and was very verbally abusive to her and the children. Even during a time we were invited to dinner at their home, he cursed at her and she was totally humiliated. We could not believe this type of treatment was coming from a pastor. He also kept weapons in the home and I am sure he threatened her that if she ever tried to leave him, he would kill her and the children. Well, long story short, she chose to stick it out and stay with him. The children have grown up and gone but she remained in the castle. Today, she is yet walking around needing healing from the years of abuse and the regrets. Why did she remain with him? There are several reasons pastors and ministers' wives or women in ministry remain in abusive situations.

False teaching is a key reason. These statements below from those in church leadership have kept abused women imprisoned in dangerous and life threatening situations for years:

"These trite phrases that clergy people offer to abused women can make life worse for the victims. Stop feeling sorry for yourself. Leave the past in the past and thank God for all your blessings. God will never give you more than you can handle. All Christians have crosses to bear. A bad husband (father) is better than no husband (father). Although the abuse is terrible, it's make you a much stronger Christian. Submit yourself totally to the will of our husband and then the abuse will stop. Go back to your husband and pray for a miracle. God calls us to be a living sacrifice. You have to work harder at being a good wife (or mother, sexual partner, etc.). Suffering builds character. Your faith in God will turn this negative experience into a positive outcome. It will save your marriage. Confess your sins and prayer harder."**16**

I believe the time is coming when we must begin to preach and teach on this subject of domestic violence in the church, from the pulpit to the door. The church has not done a very good job dealing with this "silent epidemic." We must no longer remain silent. As we teach the church that **domestic violence is a sin, it is a crime and that it is a learned behavior,** we will begin to make room in our ministries to openly discuss it, openly provide training for leaders, openly state our principles on how we must handle the abusers in our churches and how we must protect our children from repeating the cycle and becoming victims themselves. We must begin to invest in "safe housing" for those victims that need to escape to a safe place. Am I advocating breaking up homes and marriages? No, I am advocating life over death. Would you rather have a woman and children stay in a hostile environment to save the marriage and lose her life? If the church was not so "religious and pharisaical" we could really do some ministry to hurting people. I believe that God is going to release to us new strategies and power ministries to bring the giant of DV (domestic violence) to its knees.

For the past ten years, our ministries and church has flowed in deliverance ministry which includes professional counseling, special sessions for pastoral families that need deliverance and healing in these kinds of issues. We cast out of demons when needed and provide ongoing maintenance follow up. It is clear that pastoral couples need special care and they need it from leadership they can trust their lives with. Pastor's wives, minister's wives and women preachers need help. They are victims and many of them live in prisons of fear, abuse and shame. I believe the Lord has begun to locally and nationally expose this violent spirit in our churches and we had better be equipped and ready to minister to them. We need to have other support services and community services working with the church. We need training and we need it now. Some of you reading this book are victims of abuse and you have mega churches. You have money, but you don't have peace in your house. You have a big name, but you don't have anyone you can trust with your violent secret. But God is calling for truth and transparency from his leaders this hour. I can only say to those reading this book, that if you are a victim or you may be the perpetrator, your children, your seed need you to stop the vicious cycle so they will not be victims and abuse their children in the same way. The enemy wants to destroy our seed from generation to generation. I am writing this book and this chapter because I want you to know there are ministries and there are safe places for you to get support and help. I speak life and hope to you today.

"Historically, the black church has been the rock of the black community, a place of refuge where important issues are addressed. But domestic violence has long been left off the agenda, ignored in a largely patriarchal system, even justified by scripture. Now that one of the nation's most visible female evangelists(Juanita Bynum) has taken up the mantle of domestic violence, the black church has an opportunity to do something it has been criticized for not doing before: speak out on the issue and figure out how to help. "They'd tell her, 'Go back and be a good woman, be nice and make peace with him,' rather than saying, 'You deserve to be in a safe place. What he's doing is absolutely wrong'" Williams said. *17*

Bishop T.D. Jakes, Pastor of the Potter's House in Dallas, Texas, wrote a statement condemning domestic violence in the wake of the Bynum-Weeks incident, which he called "a teaching opportunity."

"The church is the place where people can find redemption even when they have made bad choices or been victims by those who did," Jakes wrote, but said that the church must do more than offer a place of refuge. We must be prepared to get the victim out of harm's way even while we are working for a solution," he wrote. "However, what the Church cannot do is to say to the victim, 'Go home and believe that God will make things better, or lead them in prayer and leave them in danger."**18**

WHAT IT'S LIKE BEING MARRIED TO A CONTROLLER/ABUSER

1. Tries to isolate her from friends, family and co-workers

2. Rigid sex roles, men are superiors and should be in charge

3. Grew up under family violence himself but didn't tell you

4. Dr. Jekyll and Mr. Hyde personality

5. Flies into rage and has an explosive temper

6. He asks like he is above the law, the church, and even God's Word

7. Personality disorder

8. Addictive behaviors (alcohol, drugs, overeating, gambling)

9. Puts blame on spouse and accepts little or no responsibility for his own behavior

10. Refuses all counseling or will choose a counselor he wants or has already influenced

11. Can be very sweet sometimes

12. Withholds affection or sex to punish you

13. Accuses you of flirting and having affairs

14. Makes you think you are crazy

15. No matter what you do, you can never make him believe you love him

16. Mistreats pets or animals

17. Threatens not to communicate

18. Cruel to her in front of others

19. Throws things, breaks things, hits, shoves and kicks partner

20. Had a parent who was abusive or a batterer

21. Wants to appear to be man of the house but she is really the backbone

22. Appears to be very religious and of great spiritual understanding but is really illiterate spiritually

23. Very nice and flirty with other women in the church but treats his wife terrible

24. Takes her money and gives her little or no money which she has earned

25. Fascination with guns or weapons and threatens her with them

26. Keeps her in check by threatening to hurt the children

27. Can be very cruel emotionally, mentally and physically

28. Neglects her basic human needs for survival

29. Has no appreciation for nice things and is destructive with things important to her

30. Will manifest strong demonic resistance to holiness and holy things such as (The Blood, the Word, prayer and fasting, worship, cleanliness, and righteous authority)

How to Help the Victims of Abuse in Your Church

1. Keep confidential matters confidential- For her protection only those trained to counsel and advise her should know and not report it back to the abuser, even if he is a member of the church. Mishandling of this information could cost her life.

2. Protect the victim (shelter or hiding place)

3. The church can provide emergency housing for her and the children as needed. The issue is safety, not anything else at the time.

4. The church can have safety kits and funds for women and children that have to flee to safety. If your church does not have a shelter, you can get her to one.

5. Work with the community resources to get the much needed services for her

6. Hold the abuser accountable but get her permission to speak to the abuser

7. Remove church leaders that are abusers until they get help, deliverance, and enroll in a program for rehabilitation.

8. Never judge the victim if they decide to leave or remain with the abuser.

We must be concerned about how we raise our sons. Because abusers are mostly male, we need to look seriously at how we rear them and if we are birthing abusers by doing the following things below:

The Making of An Abuser or Perpetrator

You are making an abuser or perpetrator when you:

1. Allow your son see his father abuse his mother over and over.

2. Never allow the son to deal with his rage that comes from not being able to rescue his mother or being beaten down by his father or the abuser while trying to rescue his mother or sister.

3. Teach boys the false doctrine that he can get away with treating women any kind of way he wants because they must submit to him no matter what he does to them.

4. Do not teach your son to love or value himself. This breeds a

man that is not capable of loving and respecting a woman as himself, and as Christ loved and gave Himself for the Church.

5. Neglect to teach him to respect and honor his mother. He will be a man that will disrespect other women as well. A man who holds his mother in high esteem usually values women.

6. Do not deal with his own sexual violations as a young boy or teen. If he never received healing or counseling for his own hurts, he may be wounded to the point of becoming a perpetrator also.

7. Ignore his addictions, (pornography and drugs) criminal behavior, or mental illness and accept it as the norm.

8. Never make him accountable for his negative actions but ignore his deviant behaviors or keep making excuses for him.

9. Continue to enable him and carry him because he is not able to keep a steady job and is not held accountable for his irresponsible behavior or non-productivity.

10. Almost always you take his side when he is accused or caught in inappropriate sexual behavior or conflicts with those in authority over him.

11. Allow him to grow up on violent and bloody movies and games and be part of a violent gang.

12. Do not monitor his friends and know who are his role models. He must be provided with positive male role models.

REFLECTIONS AND PRAYER

If this chapter was specifically for you or someone you know, pray about their freedom and deliverance from domestic violence. Share the "Letter from the Lord" with them. If God has answered your prayers and given you direction today, you must take action. Follow God's plan of escape if your spouse does not want repent and take life-long steps to change and get deliverance. Ask God for wisdom. Also make a list of all the women God has laid on your heart to pray for that are victims of some form of violence in their lives.

DEEPER REFLECTION...WHAT CAN I DO LORD?

Since reading this chapter, do you feel a calling to ministry to those in the Church that are victims of domestic violence? Is your church ready for such a ministry now? Do you have expertise, skills and resources that God can use? Do you desire to be trained in this type of ministry? Are you are survivor that wants to help other women? Write your thoughts here.

Chapter 9
_____

Single Women
Beware of Prince Charming

"Ministers need to know that perpetrators of domestic violence can be very manipulative, even charming. They will tell friends, professionals, strangers, and particularly the women they abuse exactly what the abusers think others want to hear."19

As little girls, we have been taught that one day our Prince Charming is coming to rescue us. It will be magical and marvelous and he will be the answer to all our needs. When he comes, he will sweep us off our feet. We were never taught how to discern a snake in the grass, but we were told if he goes to church, and especially if he is a preacher or man of the cloth, you can trust him. Well, that is far from true. Equally yoked is more than "he goes to church." You must be spiritually compatible and at the same level of spiritual growth to be equally yoked. Satan has fooled many of our young women and old ones too. But he particularly has traps set for women destined for greatness in God. Their "Prince Charming" is smoother than most, and is laced with abuse. For sure he will be a "controller" of her destiny, gifts and calling, money, mind and her body. If she does not comply, these men are usually on assignment to "terminate" her. Sound familiar? Well, it is time to alert women in ministry that you had better be "extra discerning" for Satan has a tailor-made prince prepared for you.

The key thing in our pastoral counseling and pre-marriage counseling that we have found is, the "controller" gains control through a "soul tie." If the woman sleeps with him (fornication) before marriage, the "controller" has legal right. Or once the marriage is consummated and final, the "controller" will really begin to manifest. There is a certain power that is given to the "controller" once the woman gives them "access to her sexual gate or makes a covenant in marriage." The assignment of Satan is to send an abuser or controller that lies dormant until his target falls into the trap. The goal is to "control and constrict" the calling of God.

My life was changed forever on the subject of *Domestic Violence* when my daughter became a victim, after only being married a few months. She was not raised in a home where there was domestic violence or name calling or fighting. I was one of those women in four that **did not** experience **domestic violence**. But it did not protect or prepare my daughter for what she experienced. The most shocking thing of all was that the young man she married professed to be a Christian and seemed to really adore her and her young son. He seemed to have a genuine respect for women, but behind closed doors he turned into "Psycho Bob."

Secondly, was the issue of her young son who was in the midst of this domestic danger. Domestic violence has a lasting and domino effect on everyone in the household. I was deeply concerned about both their safety and how the hostile environment would affect them. I soon realized that the person being violated had to make the decision to flee, not me. The victim has to realize that what was happening **was a sin, a crime, and a learned behavior. God never meant for her to be abused. It was our family prayers and support during her "terrorist marriage" that gave her the strength to flee to safety with her son.**

From experiences like this in the congregation, I began to preach from the pulpit on the silent sin called domestic violence, and the church member called Prince Charming. One in four men also in every church is an abuser waiting to strike. I want to change the way the Church thinks and ministers to those in the Body of Christ who are victims and perpetrators of domestic violence.

What is Prince Charming looking for in his victims? 20

a. Women are that needy

b. Women that are desperate to get a man

c. Women that are looking for a husband

d. Women that do not understand a criminal mind

e. Women who have problems relating to their fathers

f. Women that have stability and can take care of him (leech)

g. Women that have bad relationships with their families or no one that could protect them from him (father, brother etc.)

h. Women that are wounded and rejected

i. Women that have a strong prophetic calling on their lives

j. Women that have strong leadership giftings

k. Women that are gifted and talented and that will cover-up for the charmer's shortcomings

l. Women that are highly favored and have high visibility that could bring the abuser to the same visibility

m. Women that are beautiful who could be weakened and stripped emotionally and physically by his domination and control

n. Women who have a strong love and drive for the Lord

o. Women that are strong-willed are a challenge to him to break their will and their spirit

p. Women that are highly anointed

q. Women who are pure, so he can defile them

r. Women that are rebellious to God; his rebellious spirits are attracted to hers

s. Women who are naïve and cannot discern

t. Women who are very successful and doing great damage or have the potential to do great damage to the kingdom of darkness.

"There are battered women worshipping in our congregations. No church is abuse free, given that one of every three or four American women is abused by an intimate or former intimate partner. Christian survivors need much more than faith, prayer and positive attitude, and God to be freed from domestic violence. They also need us to stop blaming them for the abuse perpetrated upon them by their husbands and boyfriends, quit telling them that if they'd only change their behavior then marriages and families would be saved, and give them genuine love and support. They also need clergy people to realize that victims are everywhere, not just in certain cultures, races, or socioeconomic groups, nor only in urban areas." 21

How Can the Church Help Raise Awareness on Domestic
Violence?

**The Church has to talk about, teach it, preach about it and
make abusers in the church accountable for their behaviors, no
matter who they are in the church. The church must begin to
teach women and young girls how to protect themselves against
the "Prince Charming" spirit, the charmer, the chaser and the
sexual predator. The Church must teach women to discern,
denounce and seek help and deliverance from their abuser
whether it is their own father, boyfriend, husband of pastor. The
church must become a sanctuary that is a safe place from all forms
of abuse.**

"In fact, several women have told me that their pastor's responses
have stifled their healing process. Clergy say things like," You have to
work harder at being a better wife; submit yourself to your husband;
He is the head of you, as Christ is head of the church; pray so that
you'll be able to endure more pain. Remember God will never
give you more than you can bear; Divorce is a sin. You must do
everything possible to keep your family together; and the wife does
not rule over her own body, but the husband does. "22

"THIS IS BAD ADVICE AND TAKEN OUT OF CONTEXT OF SCRIPTURE. This is advice that comes from clergy that are not trained in counseling victims of domestic violence. God has called you to peace. I Cor 7:15 Marriage is sacred but so is the individual whom God created in his own image. Spousal abuse is not of God and it breaks apart women and families. Therefore it is irresponsible for clergy to pressure women into remaining in marriages that pose danger to women and children who are battered by abusive husbands."23

Just like we teach discipleship classes to new believers, we need to teach Domestic Violence 101 to both men and women, youth and children. That is one way to expose it and make the perpetrators accountable. We must give sound biblical teaching on God's view of domestic violence. We must begin training our sons very young and teach them that they must control their behavior and anger. Pastoral leaders must begin to repent and confess this sin in their own lives. Pastors will need to repent before their congregations for their sin of domestic violence. This will bring other men to repentance as well. This is what true revival will begin to look like. There is a cleansing that is coming to the House of God.

"Without training, we are prone to offer poor and insensitive pastoral care."24

Twelve Things You Need to Know About Domestic Violence [25]

1. Christian men (Church goers) are abusers to their own wives and children.

2. Many pastors and ministers are abusers to their own wives and children.

3. False church doctrine has kept many Christian women in bondage to abusive husbands and boyfriends. (Submission is abused)

4. One in every four women in church has been or is being abused.

5. A batterer (male) operates in five categories: physical beatings, verbal threats, sexual (rape), economic (taking or using her money or credit) and psychological (mind games)

6. Men who witness their parents in domestic violence are three times more likely to abuse their own wives and children.

7. An abuser operates much like a hostage taker or bank robber. He wins by taking, dominating and controlling his target. He also wins by fooling you.

8. A woman is beaten every nine seconds in America. Women ages 20-34 are the most frequently abused victims.

9. We have fooled ourselves into thinking abuse or domestic

violence does not happen in good Christian homes.

10. There is hope for the abuser and the abused. The abuser, or batterer must be willing to change behaviors, thought patterns and beliefs that have been with him their whole life. While the abuser is getting help, the abused one needs to prepare a safety plan. The abused is not at fault, but the abuser is 100% at fault.

11. We have not heard a lot of preaching on abuse from the pulpit. Maybe that's because abusers are mostly male, even though there are female abusers. Could it be that many of our male pastors are in need of deliverance and they cannot preach about those issues because they are in bondage themselves?

12. There are women that are abusive to men and their children. God frowns on this just like he does with male violence to women. Women abusers also need help in dealing with their stronghold as an abuser. There are men in the Body of Christ whose wives fight them and threaten them. Some of these women deal with bi-polar tendencies and other psychotic behaviors that are out of control.

Let's examine the signs to watch for in an abuser. Abusers can be male and female, but the dominant perpetrators happen to be male. This is the reason I believe pastors do not teach on it. Many male pastors have a problem with anger management which leads to domestic violence. Our young girls and our teen age daughters must be able to discern a prince charming spirit. We have to raise our daughters differently. They cannot grow up so sheltered and so religious that they cannot spot an imposter. She cannot be naïve and think that because a young man attends church and is a Christian, that she is safe. Quite the contrary. **Most abusers are in the church and they are in leadership positions. They are preachers, deacons, trustees, and in the back seat on the pews.** Our daughters have to be taught to discern by the Spirit, not by the outer appearance.

22 Signs of an Abuser…Prince Charming [26]

- A charmer…to charm is to seduce, cast a spell, bewitch, lure, win over, change by magic, conjure.
- Preys on women that are needy, detached and in crisis needing a Prince Charming to rescue them
- Charming but also is a hidden controller
- He say she is already in love with you, but barely knows you
- He was soooooooo nice
- Everybody liked him, he charmed them right away
- He is so attractive and normal

◆ He is tooooooooooo good to be true

◆ Uses your money and resources bringing very little to the table but he's so nice you want to help him

◆ Easily insulted... have to watch what you say

◆ EXCELLENT ACTOR...He fooled everybody, even you.

◆ Makes sure he looks totally innocent to family and friends

◆ Show emotions in extreme: may cry or be extremely controlled or have outburst of anger

◆ Usually have very low self esteem

◆ Rushes into relationships

◆ Excessively jealous as the relationships grows

◆ Has poor communication skills

◆ Blames others for his actions

◆ Addictions to drugs, porno, gambling etc.

◆ Moody

◆ Has to make most of the decisions in the relationship

◆ His ideas are always better than yours and he makes you feel stupid and inadequate

"I strongly recommend pre-marital counseling.   Our daughters and women of God need to know the person they are dating and considering for marriage at least 14-24 months.   Even if you are pregnant by him, wait.   By that time, usually all hell breaks lose

and you will find out if you are in love with a Prince Charming."

(Bishop Dr. Jackie L. Green)

As I close this chapter, it is important that we understand we can save someone's life by sharing the information in this chapter. I travel with the cd message on domestic violence so when I am prompted by the Holy Spirit, I give it to passengers as a gift. I use the cd as a witnessing tool and tell her to listen to my message on Prince Charming. I know it could save her life. It could strengthen her enough so that she would get to a safe place. It is my way of sharing the love of Jesus Christ with a battered woman and taking a risk to see her set free.

Most churches and believers don't want to get involved in domesticated issues, but I ask you, what would Jesus do? I'll tell you. He would speak truth to that battered woman and He would remind her that she was created in God's image. Jesus would tell her all about the future that He has planned for her and He would provide a way of escape. He would make visit to the perpetrator and tell the abuser of God's love for him. He would ask the abuser, why do you abuse others? And Jesus would get to the root of his problem and pull back the curtains of secrecy of abuse in the abusers own life. Jesus would tell him, "I know what you been through but there is a way, and I am that Way." Jesus would get involved and Jesus would take the risk. We must get trained and equipped to do what Jesus would do. We must protect and bring healing to hurting victims. We must challenge the abuser also and offer a way out.

We must address this "silent warfare" called domestic violence, in the parsonage, in the pulpit and in the pews.

Reflection and Prayer

Can you relate to this chapter at all from your own life or someone you know? Share how you did or almost got snared in an abusive relationship. Why would Satan want to hook you up with an abusive relationship or abusive marriage? How would that change your destiny and purpose? Do you realize that Prince Charming is a spiritual warfare tactic of Satan to destroy destiny, purpose and identity?

Chapter 10

The Silent Cry of
Preacher's Kids (PK's)

"Whenever a preacher's kid goes prodigal, we have failed them
as parents and pastors. It's time to turn our hearts back to our
children and stop sacrificing them for the sake of religion."
(Bishop Dr. Jackie L. Green)

Some of the hurt that pastor's wives and minister's wives have is because their children are the casualties of ministry. Hear the heart of my daughter, Elyzabeth Green, as she outlined and taught on some areas that preacher's kids struggle with from generation to generation. It's rare if you meet a "preacher's kid" and they are not a wounded adult that has left the church and vowed to never return. They have been silenced by the enemy and like the prodigal son, many of them have wasted their inheritance due to deep church hurts.

This chapter is dedicated on behalf of preacher's kids and the need to minister to them. Not all of them are "hurt kids," but many of them are. It is time that we begin to hear their voices and minister to them. Elyzabeth is the daughter of parents that are both preachers. Hear from her heart.

I believe somebody in the Body of Christ needs to apologize to all the preacher's kids who had great potential and destiny, but through church trauma and drama, we destroyed their potential and the desire on the inside of them, and left them as empty shells. I want to repent and apologize on behalf of the Body of Christ for how preachers kids suffered under church abuse and neglect. I believe God is about to bring restoration and healing to them so that they can arise and take their rightful places in the Kingdom of God. I believe we are coming into a great season of deliverance for pastoral families and the Body of Christ. We are about to take back what the enemy has stolen from our children in the church. Deliverance and healing begins with repentance and with confession. We must be transparent and truthful with our children and this generation. **The church must go and get their prodigal sons and daughters and "come correct" with them.**

Twelve Areas PK's Are Hurting
(By Elyzabeth Green, a PK)

1. **Don't talk, don't tell.** When there are issues in the pastor's home, you can't tell anyone at home or people in the church.

2. **You are your parent's child**. There are false expectations. You have your own calling and ministry but you are expected to be just like them and to be a carbon copy.

3. **You live in a Fish Bowl**. Your family is on always on display. Your home is the church "catch all or hotel" for everything and everybody. Hospitality is sometimes a great burden for the kids.

4. **When you mess up everybody knows**. Your mistakes are public and that it makes it harder to heal.

5. **When you mess up, your parents (the Pastor) also get the ripple effect** or the backlash.

6. **Stolen Identity:** You do not really have an identity outside of church. PK's have their identity stolen from them by the church. You can't become who God has purposed you to be, because

people put your parent's identity on your life.

7. **Church First**: You are expected to put your Pastor (father's) job first. It's not our job, that's your parent's job. I want to play sports and have recreation. We are expected to make up for the church's shortfalls. Pastoring unfortunately includes the whole family whether you volunteer or not. A lot of the PK's life is "involuntary ministry."

8. **Hear no evil, see no evil**. When the church and Pastor are in a struggle or disagreement, PK's become the whipping board. When people want to hurt your parents they make sure you to overhear their hurtful conversations, so it can wound you. (We are supposed to hear no evil, see no evil.)

9. **You cannot vent** publicly or privately. Your opinion is devalued by the church people and sometimes by your parents. You have no voice and your pain and opinion are invisible to the church.

10. **You feel uncovered.** You are left uncovered when parents defend the church, and you are hurt by a wrong or offence of church people. You feel uncovered when they choose the church over you.

11. **TIME spells LOVE.** You have to sacrifice just as much as your parents or more. You have to share your mom and dad and home. There is constant sacrifice and you have smile and be grateful. But what we really want is "time" from Mom and Pop.

12. **Many PK's are angry with God.** Neglect and anger have to be dealt with. You become angry with God when there is poverty and lack. How can we be doing so much for God and our needs are not met? Why does our family have to give up so much and suffer? Church people don't even appreciate what you have given up as PK's. **Most PK's need deliverance from anger with God, anger with the Church, and anger with their parents.**

From a parental point of view, I believe we owe the our children and especially PK's, protection even from the church. I want to share my reflections on ways to protect them following for their future inside and outside of the church.

Ten Things We Owe Our Children in Every Generation

1. **Invitation-** Extend an invitation to them to receive Jesus Christ as their Savior and Lord. (John 3:16 and I John 5:11-12)

2. **Identity**- Help them develop and discover their unique purpose in Christ and in the world. (Jeremiah 1:5, I Peter 3:9, I Corinthians 6:20)

3. **Instruction**- Disciple and teach them the Holy Scriptures and be a living example. (Isaiah 59:21, Deut. 6:7, Isaiah 28:9-10, Proverbs 22:6, Psalms 78)

4. **Involvement**- Involve them in the work of the ministry; not just toleration, but participation. (I Timothy 4:12, I Samuel 3:19-21, Luke 2:52)

5. **Intercession**- Commit to cover them in prayer and also teach how to pray.
   (I Samuel 1:27-28, Ephesians 6:10-18, II Corinthians 10:4-5, Matthew 6:5-18)

6. **Impartation**- Pass on to them the rich spiritual heritage and spiritual giftings from your life by stirring them up and pouring into them more than the milk of the Word. We must impart the meat of the Word also. (II Timothy 1:6-7)

7. **Individuality**- Help them discover and establish their

uniqueness and excitement in their own giftings, talents and future dreams and visions. Don't try to make them a clone of past generations. (Jeremiah 29:11)

8. **Influence-** Teach them to value their favor with God and people, and the influence they will have because God's Spirit will be upon them." Teach them not to abuse their influence. (Matthew 6:33 and Luke 2:52)

9. **Integrity-** We owe it to our children to people of integrity and live a life that is not fake before them. We must build trust with them, first as their parents, then as their pastors. We also must instill in them the importance of honesty, character, purity and self respect in everything they do. There is a higher standard set for them just because they are "Children of God." (Philippians 3 and 4)

10. **Inheritance-** Teach them to be proud of and protect their spiritual inheritance and not to cast their pearls to swine. (Luke 15:11-32, Ephesians 1:11, Heb.1:4)

(Photo of two of our children when they were small and quite "churched." I thank God they did not leave the church when they became young adults, but they are all in ministry and in love with Jesus today.

Don't let the church steal "their childhood.")

God will judge us if we neglect our children and the children in every generation. In Acts 8:33, the Bible says *"who shall declare his generation?"* That means that every generation will have to be accountable for it's deeds and actions. There must be someone in every generation that will be a voice for God. I Peter 2:9 says that *"we are a chosen generation and a royal priesthood."* As parents and pastors, we must make sure that our children are among the righteous and not the rebellious.

What Does God Look For in Every Generation?

1. Is the generation evil or righteous?

2. Are the prophets/my designated leaders accepted or rejected by that generation?

3. Is the generation faith filled or faithless?

4. What and who does the generation seek after?

5. Does the generation receive or reject the Son of God?

6. Does the generation tell it's children about My works and praise Me for who I am?

7. Does the generation put a high priority on procreation? (Having children and value of human life)

8. Does the generation look only for "signs?"

9. Is there a righteous remnant in that generation?

10. Is there a witness or church that I can "send" to fish in that generation and speak for Me?

I want to caution Christian parents and pastors about "never taking our children for granted." We must take time to invest in a close relationship with our kids. Many of our children were "churched" but not protected from the religious spirits that come to strip them of life and liberty. Building relationships is part of training them up in the way they should go. What good is it to grow up in church all your life and never develop a real covenant relationships with the Savior or the saints? I believe we will have to answer to God for that.

Five types of Generations the Church will have to give an account for:

1. **Ignorant Generations**- Ignorant of God the Father, Jesus the Son and the Holy Spirit *(Colossians 2:8 and Hosea 4:6, Psalms 14:1)*

2. **Idolatrous Generation**- Worshipping of false gods and false systems (Ex. 20:3-5 and I Corinthians 10:12-14)

3. **Immoral Generations**- Tolerating sexual immorality and perversion in the home, church and community *(Proverbs 30:12-13, Deut. 32:5 and Matthew 17:17)*

4. **Incarcerated Generations**- Allowing our children to fall into captivity due to sin and rebellion against God's commandments, and filling the jails and prisons with our seed. *(Genesis 18:19, Jeremiah 18:21, Jeremiah 9:20-21 and I Peter 2:13)*

5. **Irreverent Generations**-No fear of God, parents or authorities

(Psalms 78:8 and Exodus 20:7, Proverbs 30:11))

For many years and even today, my husband and I has been an advocate for children and youth in the church. Many times churches want to have a church full of children and youth, but they *don't make room* for them in programs, in ministries or allow them to be creative. My husband has cautioned church leaders and parents that we can be the reason our children leave the church if we don't listen to them or include them. We must build a strong Christian foundation but we must make room for their expressions and uniqueness. We must be tolerable of their "youthful spirits." On the other hand, we must teach them the principles for long life and success.

"Look, I am sending you the prophet Elijah before the great and dreadful day of the Lord arrives. His preaching will turn the hearts of fathers to their children, and the hearts of children to their fathers. Otherwise I will come and strike the land with a curse." Malachi 4:5-6 (NLT)

How to Make A Hoodlum (Criminal) [27]

(Copyright © 1995, Pastors Anthony and Jackie Green)

1. Don't teach them who God is or the Word of God
2. Don't teach them to respect ALL authority
3. Don't teach them to honor their mother and father
4. Don't teach the value of human life

5. Don't teach them manners and how to say "thank you"

6. Don't teach them how to forgive others and say "I'm sorry"

7. Don't teach them how to share and care for others

8. Don't teach them how to wait their turn

9. Don't teach them to never tell lies

10. Don't teach them that stealing is wrong

11. Don't teach them unconditional love

12. Don't teach them they must pay for their actions

13. Don't teach them the value of work and earning money honestly

14. Don't teach them to take a bath/shower and the importance of cleanliness and their appearance

15. Don't tell them they are special and have a God given purpose and destiny

16. Don't teach them the difference between right and wrong, or good and evil

17. Don't show them healthy boundaries in family life

18. Don't care whether they can read or write or get a good education

19. Don't teach them how to control their tongue and thought life

20. Don't lead them to salvation through Jesus Christ

21. Don't reward and encourage them, but instead abuse and criticize them.

22. Don't teach them about their ancestry or inheritance and how others paved the way for them.

I want to close this chapter by repenting to my children and all preacher's kids for the mistakes we made as parents and pastors. Our children pay a high price for parental and pastoral ignorance. I have committed the rest of my life to do whatever I can, to bring healing and restoration to the lives of pastoral families. It is time to carve out quality time to minister to our children; to have conferences and retreats for them; to create relevant curriculum for them; to offer deliverance and healing ministry to them, just like we have done for ourselves. I want to make sure there are no more generations of "prodigal preacher's kids." We must go and get our prodigal sons and daughters, and bring them home; wash and bandage them; do the necessary spiritual warfare over them that we should have done; and believe God will restore them and restore our relationships with them. Every church needs to repent to it's young people from time to time to bring about the cleansing needed in the Body of Christ today. This will be one of the signs of true revival.

Reflection and Prayer

List the names of all the preacher's kids you know. Pray for them and ask the Lord how you can minister to them. Find time to have open discussion with your children about areas of hurt and pain in their lives. It's never too late to allow the Lord to heal those wounds in their lives and release them into what God has called them to do.

Chapter 11

Witchcraft...What You Don't Know Can Hurt You

Out of all the chapters in the book, this chapter is the most hated by the Devil. This chapter will confront the invisible realm that we don't readily see operating in our churches today. It is an area that the "religious folk" don't like to talk about. It is a great area of "ignorance" in the Church today. I am addressing witchcraft because it was very instrumental in me being a "Hurt Lady." In my first few years of being young pastor's wife, I got my first education in witchcraft in a small family church. One of the elderly church mothers told me things most folk would not dare speak of. She would come to me and share with me church history and the things that she felt kept the church from growing all those years, and the things that ran pastors away, even suicide in the parsonage. The church could not keep a pastor and of course there were many wounded "First Ladies." I asked the Lord, why was she coming to me? He told me to *"Listen and learn, because this was a realm the church and many former pastoral families had ignored."* The calling on my life would require me knowing such information and coming into a revelation of the unseen world of the kingdom of darkness. God was going to use me to bridge many gaps and break open truth that had been hidden, and to teach and bring God's people into present truths that had been destroying the church for years.

WITCHCRAFT IS ALL AROUND US. We have to preach and teach about it. We are not to be consumed with it, but we had better stop being ignorant of the devil's devices in the Church. The Apostle Paul had to deal with witchcraft in the early churches by believers and non-believers that dabbled in it. What is witchcraft?

"Witchcraft has its roots in rebellion. It is the root of all human problems. Rebellion and witchcraft are twins." **28** (I Samuel 15:23)

"God's highest purpose is not to humiliate the wizard or the witch, but to convert him to Jesus Christ. This is not to bless what they are doing, but to bless them, and pray for them and their souls. Blessings are more powerful than curses. Witchcraft is basically the practice of cursing others. Witchcraft is the manipulation, or control spirit, regardless of who it comes through."**29**

The Word of God gives of clear direction as to the origin of witchcraft and why it is forbidden.

"When thou art come into the land which the LORD thy God giveth

thee, thou shalt not learn to do after the abominations of those nations.

There shall not be found among you [any one] that maketh his son or

his daughter to pass through the fire, [or] that useth divination, [or] an

observer of times, or an enchanter, or a witch, or a charmer, or a consulter

with familiar spirits, or a wizard, or a necromancer. For all that do

these things [are] an abomination unto the LORD: and because of these

abominations the LORD thy God doth drive them out from before thee.

Thou shalt be perfect with the Lord thy God." Deuteronomy 18:9-13

(KJV)

"O foolish Galatians, who hath bewitched you, that ye should not

obey the truth, before whose eyes Jesus Christ hath been evidently set forth,

crucified among you?" Galatians 3:1 (KJV)

"But if ye be led of the Spirit, ye are not under the law. Now the

works of the flesh are manifest, which are [these]; Adultery, fornication,

uncleanness, lasciviousness, Idolatry, witchcraft, hatred, variance,

emulations, wrath, strife, seditions, heresies, envyings, murders,

drunkenness, revellings, and such like: of the which I tell you before, as I

have also told [you] in time past, that they which do such things shall not inherit the kingdom of God."   *Galatians 5:19-31 (KJV)*

Pastoral families have not been equipped to recognize or combat witchcraft in the pews. There surely was no training in seminary. We have walked blindly into churches and tried to pastor them, not discerning the workings of witchcraft were heavy at work. What we did not know and what we were ignorant of had the power to destroy our marriage and ministries.

Please refer to the *Occult and New Age Terms* in the Appendix section to help you understand some of the terminology that I will be using throughout the book. The word list of terms will help pastoral leaders and church leadership add to their arsenal of spiritual warfare language.

Before I share with you the warning signs of witchcraft, I want you to know that if we listen to the Holy Spirit, there is much He is willing to teach us. When we arrived at our first pastorate some twenty five years ago, there were probably about twenty people in the congregation. The church looked empty and felt abandoned. Every morning at 6:00a.m. I would meet the Lord at the church to pray. The Holy Spirit spoke to me one morning and said: *"Look in the midst. There are more demons seated in those pews and on the church roll than saints. I will teach you how to empty out the pews of the "congregation of demons" and then you will begin to see church growth."* I believed the Lord point blank. I knew then that spiritual warfare is not about what you see in the natural, but it's about the unseen, which is more real than the people sitting in the pews.

Now let's examine some warning signs of witchcraft that might be at work in your marriage, family and church. Everything that I am sharing with you comes from my own personal experience and what the Holy Spirit has taught about spiritual warfare. But for sure everything that is happening to you or your ministry is "not a demon." But you must have discernment and the gift of discerning of spirits working in your life to discern the difference.

"Discerning of spirits is the supernatural ability to recognize and distinguish between not only good and bad, but various classes of spirits: The Holy Spirit, Good angels, fallen angels, demons or evil spirits and the human spirit. Sometimes when dealing with the spiritual realm, we can find ourselves facing "gray" areas where things are unclear. That is one time when we need the gift of discerning of spirits to clear away the gray and separate matters into black and white?"**30**

25 Warning Signs that Witchcraft Might Be At Work In the Midst of the Pastoral Family and Church

1. **Psychic or Demonic prayers**- prayers that are being prayed to manipulate the pastor and family or the church leadership by disgruntled and rebellious members or outside forces. Also prayers that pray directly against the Word of the Lord and the well being of the pastor, his wife, children and the church. Beware of prayers that are prayed against the vision and success of the ministry.

2. **Financial Lack and Pressures**- Extreme warfare over the financial well being of the pastor and family by control of the church leadership and withholding of that which rightly belongs to the Pastor and family. Sabotage of pastor's benefits and livelihood. The Pastoral family is tithing and giving out but there is a hold up on what is rightly earned or sense of financial obstruction demonic interference.

3. **Control and manipulation**- Beware of money and gifts given to the First Family and church by those that are well off or wealthy. Some persons will give to the pastor to later put demands for priority treatment or manipulation and threaten to withdraw their financial support if they do not get their way. All money must be prayed over

and curses broken off, and then consecrated to the Lord. All money is not "good money."

4. **Cursed Food**- People cooking for the First Family and putting potions or herbal magic over the food to accomplish witchcraft. Always watch what you eat and where you eat.

5. **Delivered Curses through Gifts**- Beware of gifts, artifacts and fetishes in your home that were given to you by those that have actually cursed you and the objects. Pray over all gifts and ask the Lord to reveal the "spirit behind the gifts."

6. **Sudden Illness and physical attacks** - Don't panic, but be alert to sudden illness, chronic illness, accidents, financial ruin, and when your marriage begins to come under strange attacks. Constant miscarriages, unexplained illnesses, cars breaking down or trouble keeping and getting a car. This is indication that there may be curses in motion.

7. **Relationship Warfare**-Sudden or unexplained relationship problems, arguments, fights and hostile spirits released in the household. Thoughts of separation and divorce, and pressure in the marriage has increased. Children are fighting and have become

rebellious and distant. Family communication has been majorly disrupted.

8. **Unexplained desires and vain imaginations-** Mental warfare being waged and the mind is being bombarded with vain imaginations, demonic dreams and thoughts. The pastor's wife or the pastor cannot explain why they are being enticed by other men and women in the congregation or outside the church to cause them to fall into sexual sin. Scandal has been released against the pastoral family and it comes through witchcraft and the power of suggestion.

9. **Spirits of slander-**Character assassination and demonic plots or conspiracies begin to circulate, and demonic magnification is released against the pastor or pastor's wife which is the spirit of the false witnesses and false accusations.

10. **Controlling Families in the Church** - Blocking spirits through controlling families are released to hinder progress for years to stop progress and growth of the pastoral leadership. Witchcraft is seen working through controlling and power hungry families in the church that have been part of Satan's plan to stop progress. These families defend family members above authority and God's order and will fight for controlling power.

11. **Covens at work**- Watch out for strange prayer groups and strange Bible studies that are popping up unauthorized in the church. These are signs that infiltration is coming in, and many times these groups are not under the authority of leadership. Witchcraft is at work. Confront it. These covens pray against the vision and plants seeds of discord.

12. **Spirit of Python**- A spirit of divination that is released against the pastoral family and the church. You feel that something is squeezing you, putting pressure and suffocating your finances and resources. You begin to feel your hopes, faith and visions and dreams will not succeed. You know you are in warfare and it is a life and death struggle to survive.

13. **Loss of Concentration**- It is hard to study, concentrate and focus on the things of God. There are those that are praying against the pastor's mind.

14. **False Words and False Prophecy**-False flattery is spoken to the Pastor and wife but it was really the backstabber trying to gain entry. Beware of those that prophesy over you or your children without your permission. This is how witchcraft enters and false words enter your spirit, which can cause infirmity and torment.

15. **Laying on of Hands**-Be careful who lays hands on you and your children. There is a transference that takes place with the laying on of hands and witchcraft can be sent through the laying on of hands. Guard your children and those who pray for them. Curses are released to the head (your authority), your shoulders (governmental rule) and your belly, (where your rivers of living water are stationed) when hands are laid on those body parts.

16. **Befriending the Children**- Satan will assign people to allure your children by buying the children things and going behind the parents back doing things with the children the parents would not allow or tolerate. Beware of adult members that get to be friends with kids as a gateway to the pastor's home and family and using the children as informats.

17. **False armor bearer or servant**-False servants are sent to serve the pastor's wife or pastor and to infiltrate the pastoral family and plant deception and division. The spirit of the charmer and forked tongue (flattery) is how they bewitch the pastor's wife into believing everything they say and do because she is lonely and the pastor is gone most of the time. These false servants can also release a marriage breaking spirit and home wrecker spirit because they have access to the pastor's and wife's private life and home. One that is single,

available, secretly bitter, seductive and jealous of the Pastor's wife can appear to be the ideal armor bearer. Don't choose an armor bearer too quickly. You will regret it.

18. **Potions, Perfumes, Powders**-The three P's (potions, perfumes, powders) and even lotions given to the pastor and wife but they cursed the items. Be careful. If you get a check in your spirit, throw it out. Candles and jewelry are things that are personal and can be inhaled and jewelry can be cursed. Be mindful of wall paintings and pictures that may have things planted within the frames to bring curses. Remember some curses are sent and other curses must be delivered to you.

19. **Hair Stylist**-Being careful who does your hair. If they are on an demonic assignment, they can perform rituals with your (cut) hair. I did experience this and felt the Lord cautioned me to change hairdressers. I did not heed His Voice. Seven days later, all my hair began to fall out and I began having trouble with that beautician. I never went back.

20. **Blood line curses** -Study your own family history and know what bloodline curses and what bloodline blessings are in your family tree. Sometimes what you are going through is due to the sins of the father

and your mother. Study your history and study the church history to see what has been set in motion.

21. **Evil Eye**- These are women in the church that envy and are jealous of the pastor's wife and send curses through a "look that could kill." This is a cockatrice spirit that kills with a glance, or evil eye. *See Appendix E for definitions.*

22. **Seedings and workings**- Things planted in the parsonage or the church grounds to attract demonic activity and to curse the property. Walk the church property and parsonage ground regularly and pray and anoint it. Draw a line in the Spirit and forbid witchcraft activity to operate. Dead animals, powdery substances, feathers or coins left in formations could mean curses have been released.

23. **Freemasons**- Churches that have been founded by Freemasons as former pastors or founding members bring upon that church curses that hinder growth and revival, and these strongholds fight against anyone that comes in to raise up a standard of holiness. Secret societies are secret because there are areas of darkness that are hidden. Occult means hidden. Many churches historically are tied up in freemasonry and there are levels that the church cannot reach spiritually until there is repentance and denouncing of all occult

allegiances and demonic covenants.

24. Demonic visitations- Visitations in the parsonage, particularly in
the form of terror by night, where there are demonic manifestations
in the house to frighten you or to let you know you have shaken
the kingdom of darkness. No need to fear, just declare the Blood
and Psalms 91 as you walk through your home and command those
evil spirits to leave. Ask God to release His angels of protection and
warring angels to do battle with you.

25. Jezebel Spirit - Seduction and sabotage of the pastor's marriage
and family even if it takes five, ten, or fifteen years to carry out their
demonic assignment. There are assignments set in place to cause
destruction and these are called "marriage breaking spirits or "home
wrecker spirits." Where you find the Jezebel spirit in a church, you
will find witchcraft in operation, undermining authority in the
church, especially male authority.

15 Things that Keep Witches From Infiltrating God's House

1. Keep true to your *First Love*– Jesus Christ.
2. Know the power of the Blood of Christ and how to appropriate
   it.
3. The church must operate in true five fold leadership that is

functioning and discerning those false influences such as false prophets, false doctrine and the spirit of error, as well as witchcraft and occult activity. Many churches today has fought against the ministry of the apostles and prophets. But apostles and prophets are arch warriors that God used to spot and expel witchcraft and divination in the Early New Testament Church. We need those five fold giftings in the church today.

4. Releasing the fire of the Lord in intercession, prophetic worship, Prophetic declaration and the fire of God's love.

5 Be filled with the Holy Spirit and evidence of the Fruits of the Spirit

6. Be a house of prayer with consistent, strategic, fervent intercession.

7. Be firm and mature in your discernment and discerning of spirits.

8. Be discerning and disciplining of **all** sexual sins in the congregation.

9. Be careful to observe and screen potential leaders that could be implants sent to infiltrate and bring division and sexual scandal.

10. Keep a true spirit of repentance operating in the church.

11. Flow in the true spiritual gifts which will expose the false gifts.

12. Train your leaders to operate in and judge prophecy in the church.

13. Teach and train how to identify witchcraft and the occult so the

church can discern it, confront it and begin to war against it.

14. Cast out devils, rebuke and subdue the powers of darkness in your city and region.

15. Teach your leaders to pay attention to details in the midst. Most of our leaders and congregation are very unaware of their surroundings and those that are around us while at church.

Seven Weapons that Never Fail Against Witchcraft

1. **The Power of the Blood** - Know and declare and decree the power of the Blood of Jesus Christ which has the power of salvation, redemption, healing and protection for those that receive it and appropriate it. *(Rev. 12:11)*

2. **The Power of the Word** - Study, decree, declare and live by the Word of as a sure weapon against that which is false. *(Proverbs 30:5, Jer. 23:29-30)*

3. **The Power of Christ' Name** - Declare and decree the name of Jesus Christ of Nazareth, the Son of the Living God, the King of Kings and the Lord of Lords; His Name is above every name, and every knee must bow and every tongue confess His Lordship. *(Philippians 2:10-11)*

4. **Power of the Keys of the Kingdom** - Execute the power given to us by Christ to bind and to loose in the earth and in

heaven. This includes the power to bind demonic kings with fetters of iron. *(Matthew16:19)*

5. **The Power to Discern** - Use the weapons of discernment and discerning of spirits to know what type of spirits and forces that are in operation. This includes discerning the intents of people and their motives. *(Hebrews 4:12)*

6. The **Power of Prayer** - The ability to pray with understanding and pray in your prayer language. Praying with all types of prayers led by the Holy Spirit. Praying without ceasing. *(Ephesians 6:10-17)*

7. **The Fear of the Lord** - is a weapon against witchcraft that will keep you obedient to all the commands of the Lord, but you will also release a fear into the enemy's camp. There is a spirit of wisdom and revelation released with the fear of the Lord that is vital in dealing standing against witchcraft and the occult. *(Isaiah 11:2, Psalms 27:l, Proverbs 29:25 and Proverbs 1:7))*

FIRST AID

Reflection and Prayer: WITCHCRAFT...
WHAT YOU DON'T KNOW CAN HURT YOU!

1. Take this time to journal and reflect on the times that you probably were experiencing witchcraft in the church, in your family or your marriage.

_____

_____

_____

_____

2. **What ways could you have protected yourself better from witchcraft?**

_____

_____

_____

_____

3. How will you educate your children or even the church about the dangers of witchcraft and rebellion? _____

_____

_____

_____

4. Have you ever taught or preached on witchcraft and the occult? What?

_____

_____

_____

_____

5. Were there times the Holy Spirit warned you to be more alert and discerning, but you were gullible and allowed yourself to be deceived?

_____

_____

_____

_____

6. Have there been times that you discerned things and warned your husband or the Pastor?_____

_____

_____

_____

How discerning has he been in the area of witchcraft and the occult influences in your midst? Why must you BOTH be more equipped than the congregation in this area?

Chapter 12

The Hurt Lady Pastor

"While he was still talking with them, Rachel came with
her father's sheep, for she was a shepherdess."
Genesis 29:9(NIV)

"It was He who gave some to be apostles, some to be
prophets, some to be evangelists, and some to be pastors and
teachers, to prepare God's people for works of service, so that the
body of Christ may be built up until we all reach unity in faith
and in the knowledge of the Son of God and become mature,
attaining to the whole measure of the fullness of Christ."
Ephesians 4:11-13 (NIV)

"And the apostle Paul mentions a total of seven women when
listing his trusted co-laborers. These were women who functioned as
pastors, evangelists, deacons or apostles. It seems odd that Christian
men would have difficulty accepting the authority of women when

every man has had to submit to the instruction and discipline of his own mother." **31**

If you are a woman and you have had children, you know what the labor room is like. One thing a woman never wants to experience is "being in the labor room alone." Birthing a baby alone can be dangerous, but most of all, intensely lonely. Birthing is filled with psychological warfare that is hard to describe in words. Husbands who have been in the labor room with their wives know what tremendous mental and emotional support a woman needs when birthing a child. However, history has recorded that there are women who have had to bring a baby into the world alone. They dealt with the contractions, they had to push and cut the umbilical cord too. It was hard. It was emotionally stressful, but her main concern is "is my baby alright?" There have been women who have birthed with just a midwife present, and thank God for that. ***A woman in labor needs support for her and the baby.***

What I have just described is what it's like to be a female pastor in many regions of our nation today. She is left to birth a church or ministry and oversee it alone. If she births her ministry in the "Bible Belt," she is most likely to be whipped for it while she is in labor. Once the baby comes forth, no one wants to step forward and embrace the newborn. She is very much pastoring as an outcast and the fruit of her labor and ministry is disdained and discarded by those who do not acknowledge her pastorate as a female shepherd. She can have all the qualifications, and even more qualified than a male pastor- but because of her gender and because of traditions and twisted interpretations of scripture, she and her ministry grow up in the Body of Christ under the stronghold of discrimination and excommunication.

The Bible tells us that Rachel was a shepherdess. I chose this text because in the natural realm, we know shepherds to be traditionally males but we see that women could also hold that position. Rachel was beautiful, but she had to be able to do what shepherds do, not based on her gender, but based on skill, wisdom, experience and invested authority. According to biblical history and understanding of the duties of a shepherd, it is clear the duties are not based on gender: The shepherd/shepherdess duties were to:

1. Guard the sheep in the wilderness from wolves and predators
2. Anoint the heads of sheep with oil to preserve them from sunstroke, or to heal scratches from bushes and injuries.
3. Rescue and defend the flock or a sheep from dangerous situations
4. Count the sheep, and keep record and give an account to the master

5. Fleece the sheep for sheepskin for coats for themselves

6. Lead the flock to green pastures and find fresh drinking water

7. Guide the flock to a peaceful valley to rest and lie down

8. Feed the sheep

9. Carry those sheep or lambs back to the flock that have strayed away

10. Carry the staff as a weapon against the wolves and to tap the rocks at night by making a sound to let them know the shepherd is near.

11. Speak to sheep, for the sheep know the voice of their shepherd.

12. Comfort the sheep with his/her rod and staff which guides and protects them.

A female pastor is a *shepherdess, and* must know that she is carrying out the duties of a true shepherd whether she is accepted or not. She must obey the Lord and be accountable for the sheep she has been given oversight of. Healing comes to shepherdesses because they draw from the wells of "Salvation of the Savior" and not from the wells of traditions of men.

It is important for the shepherdess to remember and obey the directives they received from the Chief Shepherd, Jesus Christ.

"Keep watch over yourselves and all the flock of which the Holy Spirit has made you overseers. Be shepherds of the church of God, which he bought with his own blood. I know that after I leave, savage wolves will come in among you and will not spare the flock. Even from your own number men will arise and distort the truth in order to draw away disciples after them" Acts 20:28-30 (NIV)

There is first aide care for the female shepherd. I want to suggest these Twelve Commandments for Women Pastors from my own years of experience and from my healing process that the Lord has taken me through.

12 Commandments for Women Pastors

1. Thou shall not try to dress, act, or shepherd like a man. You shall be beautiful and feminine.
2. Thou shall not discriminate against other women or male shepherds, nor compare yourself to them.
3. Thou shall love, respect and pray for those leaders in the Body of Christ that hate women pastors and call you a cult or witch. Instead, let God use you to break down barriers and bring reform and revelation to your region and city.

4. Thou shall shepherd My people with excellence and do all in within your power and authority to execute your duties.

5. Thou shall forgive those that discriminate and slander both you and the ministry I have given to you.

6. Thou shall be an example to the sheep and other shepherds of how to walk in integrity, equality and true spiritual authority.

7. Thou shall lay your life down for the sheep, giving your all, and never abusing the sheep for personal gain and filthy lucre.

8. Thou shall not war against the people (flesh-and-blood enemies) but against evil rulers and authorities of the unseen world, against mighty powers in this dark world, and against evil spirits in the heavenly places.

9. Thou shall not hold back or draw back because of the fear of man, fear of religion or traditions of men, but shall press forward to the high calling that is upon your life.

10. Thou shall be ready to give an answer of the faith and calling that is within you and defend the Gospel of Jesus Christ, and not become entangled in "arguments and ancient strongholds" of religious ignorance against women in the Body of Christ.

11. Thou shall get ongoing biblical counseling, healing and deliverance for your own personal hurts and strongholds.

12. Thou shall keep yourself accountable to both male and

female righteous leadership as you develop your pastoral leadership skills so that you will not fall into error, pride and sin.

Psychological Warfare is Different for Female Pastors

I believe that 80% of pastoring and serving in leadership roles involves "psychological warfare." The wear and tear on the mind is tremendous. Most pastors, male and female, leave the ministry because they were overtaken in by "mental warfare." *They were "psyched out" by the enemy from years of mental warfare and strain.*

Psychological Warfare is one of the oldest weapons in the arsenal of man and Satan. It is a war of the mind. It is a strong form of demonic mind control. Satan sends information to us through repetition, torment, breaking team morale, the power of persuasion, isolation and intimidation to get us to surrender. Then the enemy will laugh and release shame and disgrace and declare that God of Heaven was not able to keep us. The goal of these attacks on your mental processes, emotions, mental recall, attitude and behavior is to wear you down and get you to surrender without a fight if possible. Satan has long-term warfare package, in which he orchestrates years of planned attacks on your mind.

Psychological tests suggest that women have a greater tolerance for pain, and even live longer and are more resistant to disease than men. But psychological warfare for women in ministry is different because she has to contend not only with the saints for preaching the Gospel and ushering in the Kingdom, but she has gender hater demons" assigned to her. She has an arch enemy, that old serpent, that has hated her since the time of the Fall of Man.

"And I will cause hostility between you and the woman, and between your offspring and her offspring. He will strike your head, and you will strike his heel." Genesis 3:15 (NLT)

Psychological warfare is mental warfare and she must learn how to protect her sanity, quiet her mind, cast down imaginations, silence the voices of the enemy; and not believe the lies!

SATAN'S GOAL- To psyche you out so bad that you surrender, quit, throw in the towel, accept defeat, and/or accept automatic failure.

GOD'S GOAL- To teach us how to totally depend on Him and know that He will defend us and protect us no matter how the odds are stacked against us. God will not remove the warfare, but He will give us victory over it.

14 Familiar Psychological Warfare Strategies

Here are some principles we can use from King Hezekiah as he was in great psychological warfare. Much of the warfare that pastors go through is mental warfare. Mental warfare is meant to wear us down. Women however have additional "mental warfare" and must be prepared for it.

1. Isaiah 36:5- Satan discredits the Word of God and says the Word is not reliable enough to stand on. He attacks your faith in God. **He makes you question whether or not you really heard from God.**

2. Isaiah 36:7- Satan discredits your faith and belief in the Lord. Satan will mock your obedience to God. He will also want to keep you hidden and measure your "fame." **Satan fights you and all avenues toward you becoming known and successful.**

3. Isaiah 36:9- Satan mocks our small resources, our tiny army and our weaknesses. Satan measures your finances and means of resources. **He wants you to equate your success by making you measure and compare yourself and your finances against other ministries and their finances.**

4. Isaiah 36:12- Satan paints a picture of the worst case scenario

possible that could happen to us. **He wants to measure your influence and make you think that you have no influence in your city or region or nation.**

5. Isaiah 36:13- Satan speaks against spiritual leadership and the church when things are going bad in our lives. He makes us think our people or church or ministry think we are deceiving them. **He comes against those that are loyal to you and attacks them. Satan brings in pain and shame to us through discord, division, departure and desertion.**

6. Isaiah 36:16- "Open the gates and come out." Satan's real goal is to defeat you and get you to leave your assignment or ministry. Leave the Lord, leave it all, and take Satan's false offers . He wants you to think the grass is greener and the bread and wine is sweeter over there. **Satan wants to displace you.**

7. Isaiah 36:21- Watch your words and statements in time of psychological warfare. Satan tried to get the people to talk back or talk against Hezekiah. But the people remained silent and did not answer him. We don't need to answer Satan or engage him in conversation. Watch your mouth in this season. **Watch who you confide in because the same folk that flatter you will be the same**

ones that will crucify you.

8.   Isaiah 37:5- Hezekiah sought out the wisdom and instruction from the Prophet Isaiah. The Prophet predicted the enemy's fall. Satan wants to isolate you, but that is the time to get wise counsel. **Seek counsel from the apostles and prophets of the Lord.**

9. Isaiah 37:14- King Hezekiah spread out the insults and threatening letters from the enemy before the Lord. Hezekiah prayed and fasted and consulted the Lord of Heaven's Armies. (This is key… you don't need to always answer the phone or the front door.) The enemy wanted the King to come out and the enemy wanted to get the King out of position. But Hezekiah got attacks the people did not get. Leaders get attacks others do not get. The enemy WILL SUMMON YOU BECAUSE HE WANTS TO STRIP YOU. **Pray and fast in times of great mental warfare. Discern which battles you are to fight and which battles are the Lord's.**

10. Isaiah 37:36- That night the angel of the Lord went out to the Assyrian camp and killed 185,000 Assyrian soldiers. When the Assyrians woke up the next morning, they found corpses everywhere. **Satan makes you forget you have angelic help and assistance. God will send you angelic help.**

**We must learn how to call on the "Lord of Heaven's Armies",
Jehovah Saboath, in times of mental warfare.**

11. Isaiah 38:1--Hezekiah's body became deathly ill, but he prayed
and did recover. I believe this illness is a physical manifestation of
the prolonged psychological warfare. **Take care of your body. Satan
wants to break down your body and bring sickness, infirmity, and
finally death. Take time for a "selah" or even a vacation. Warfare
is work. Eat properly, sleep and rest but also find time to have
fun. Balancing the pastoral ministry keeps us from breaking
down in our mind, body and spirit.**

12. II Chronicles 32:5 --**Repair all the broken sections** in the walls
of your life and ministry. When the mental warfare is so strong and
you've done all you can, check yourself and see if there are gaps in
your fortress. Do a self evaluation and make sure there is no sin or
areas of disobedience in your life or in the ministry.

13. Matthew 14:50- When you are deserted and spurned by
those you trusted, served and labored with, remember this is part of
shepherding. Successful shepherding means enduring and taking the
bitter with the sweet. Jesus our Lord was also deserted by those close
to Him.

14. II Timothy 4:10- There will always be thieves and robbers of the gifts and calling. They just want ministry validation but they don't want real covenant relationships. This can wound us especially when they have been in the midst of you for five to ten years. When you are a female pastor and God has given you favor and a "name," struggling women will be drawn to you and those that are sent to pimp you for their purposes. Some will have no loyalty or allegiance to you but come to steal from the ministry and then go out as a false witness against the ministry. They want to use your name but want no accountability. **Even so, God calls us to not become hardened and not to shut down on helping others. We must become more discerning in testing the spirits and become better judges of character and motives.**

Identifying the 12 Major Areas of Hurt for Female Pastors

1. Rejected for being a female with a pastoral calling. We cannot change who God made us nor can we spend the rest of our lives under the curses of "gender haters."

2. Rejected by spiritual leaders that we once served. It is devastating to be rejected by those you labored with and then cast aside because you became a shepherdess.

3.   Excommunicated from churches and denominations who can no longer control your destiny and who fear you will take their members. Many of these churches pimped you but would not promote you.

4.   When your husband is supportive but he is now rejected and excommunicated by his friends and the "good old boys" because of your position as pastor or co-pastor.

5.   When you are the co-pastor with your husband and he pacifies you with a title, but you have no authority or real designated place. You are just the "clean up" woman. You do what is left over to do, but you are never considered valuable enough to be paid or com-pensated for your skills, education or expertise. Basically, you are also being used by your husband and the church.

6.   Rejected and disrespected by women in the church who see you as a "Jezebel" or one that is stepping into an arena that is only "for males."

7.   The psychological warfare that comes from the region or city against female pastors is directed through demons and territorial spirits of resistance. This mental warfare is real and if the shepherdess is not strong in spiritual warfare, she will succumb to the demonic attacks and eventually quit the ministry, become sick and depressed, or become a very "bitter

pastor."

8. The Body of Christ will accept a corrupt, unqualified male shepherd quicker than they will receive a holy, qualified female shepherdess with a proven ministry.

9. Lack of emotional and financial support from friends, family and colleagues in times of spiritual transition and change.

10. Loneliness in the ministry. Women clergy and especially female pastors are geographically scattered and many times have no communication with other female pastors in their own region for months or even years. They yearn for a "sister pastor" relationship but there are very few.

11. Betrayal and sabotage by those you trusted and poured into their lives. They will pull from your ministry, get validation, and leave to go out and slander you. Some go back to those churches and pastors that you protected and healed them from and brought them into their calling. Even betrayal by other women pastors you trusted with your ministry and people, who turned and scorned you because of jealousy.

12. Curses of "Automatic Failure" released against her by those who have no discernment or understanding of the calling and the price she must pay to obey God. These curses are spoken by family, friends, churches, and other pastors that do not

understand Kingdom building. They don't realize that we are all "on the same team." If women pastors fail, we all fail. We are One Body. When one part of the Body hurts, we all hurt. Female pastors struggle constantly with curses released against them to cause them to fail in Kingdom work.

I want to close this chapter by just reminding women that are yet called to pastoral positions and leadership to remember

14 Keys to Success in Leadership [32]

1. Remember pastoring or leadership is not for cowards. (II Timothy 1:7)

2. Your reward comes from God. (Hebrews 6:10)

3. Remember: Jesus was also rejected and despised by men. (Isaiah 53:3)

4. Pioneer and pave the way for our daughters so they will have it better than we did and teach them how to pray and tell them how you overcame. (Jeremiah 9:20 and Psalms 121)

5. Let your journey experiences make you better, not bitter. (Hebrews 12:15, and Ephesians 4:31)

6. Live your life as one that has a "sent one's" attitude and commission from God. (Matthew 28:18-20 and Mark 16:15-

20)

7. Nothing can stop us and none of these things move us, for the Spirit of the Lord is upon us, and is with us. What can man do to us? We have the victory and the acceptance by our Lord already. (Romans 9:28-39 and Acts 20:24)

8. War against the enemy but don't forget to worship the Lord ! (Psalms 149:6-9)

9. Be quick to forgive those that hurt you (Ephesians 4:31-32)

10. Study and prepare yourself for your mission. (II Timothy 2:15)

11. Mentor and encourage another "sistah pastor" or sister-in-Christ along the way. (I Corinthians 4:15)

12. Keep your eyes on the Master and the mission! (Philippians 4:13-14)

13. Bless your enemies, don't bash. (Matthew 5 :44)

14. Keep an open door of reconciliation to preachers, pastors, spiritual prodigal sons and daughters that abandoned you and deserted you. (II Cor. 5:18)

Reflection and Prayer: The Hurt Pastor

Journal in this section the feelings that have been stirred as we talked about the hurts and the twelve commandments. What is God saying to you in this season of your ministry as a *female pastor*? If you are not a female pastor, share your feeling here on how you can pray for women in senior leadership roles.

Chapter 13

---

30 Struggles of Women in Ministry

"Try to build up and not tear down your sister in ministry. There is enough struggle already without struggling with another sister. Do not allow men to put your sisters down publicly or privately. Thou shall not let jealousy of another sister's gift make you miss a blessing. Thou shall celebrate a sister's gift." 33

There are many hurting women in ministry and in the church today. They just want to follow Jesus and obey the call of God upon their lives. They did not know there would be so many struggles and strategic plots against them. But we know in life that anything worth having or accomplishing does not come without a struggle. I love the words and in the Random House Roget's Thesaurus, the word "struggle" means: to battle, fight, contend, exchange blows, work hard, move heaven and earth, labor, strain, lock horns, oppose forces, long haul, push and war. Sounds like the life of the woman called by God and what she must do to step into purpose and destiny.

Satan is not going to just let you walk into it, but you and I will have to contend for our rightful position in Christ. Our positioning is already granted by the Master, but we still must contend with demonic forces in our homes, churches, cities, regions and nations.

In my struggle with opposing forces. I realize that those struggles have made me mature and made me wiser. A woman in ministry or a preacher's wife lives a life of "showdowns." She has to stand firm in the face of the devil and in the face of church folk. It's always a showdown between God's Word and the word of the nay sayers. As women of God, we must be ready to live on the cutting edge but also know that every showdown is an opportunity for growth and victory.

I want to say here also how much I love my husband and how he stood with me through the years of struggle as a woman that was the first one licensed in a 100 year old church and later I was the first one to be ordained It was a season of showdowns with stubborn denominational districts and conventions; with mean and controlling church leaders; spiritual illiteracy among church leaders regarding what the Bible really says about women in authority and leadership; with women in the background who were fearful and did not have enough backbone to value themselves, and know that my warfare would open the way to their liberty and freedom. Many sisters "sat on the fence" as I went through the fire. And today, some of them are in the ministry and have been licensed and ordained because I went through the fire and was not afraid of a "righteous showdown."

It is important for me to say that I will always honor and respect my husband who stood with me; and he took some hits too. Every time I was thrust forward in God, my home and marriage had to make adjustments. I remember during those times of transition, the word was out that I was licensed. Many churches no longer wanted to fellowship with our church. And when we did attend services at those churches, my husband would not sit in the pulpit unless I could sit with him. It made a powerful statement to those who had never seen real "team ministry." It was a struggle, but I have no regrets.

Marriage, motherhood, and ministry is not for cowards. You had better get ready for the struggle, but also the victory! It's not a new struggle for women, just because you answered your calling. No, we have been in this struggle since the Garden of Eden.

" Satan hates women with a great wrath. One way you can always determine the level of the anti-Christ spirit and his operations is how you see the women being treated in a region. Similarly, how you see women being treated in the Church, displays the level of freedom of God in that region. The two are in direct correlation with each other."34

"We will not win the war of the Church without women coming into place for what God is doing this hour. Now is the time dear sisters for you to understand your invaluable worth, come into alignment with what God has for you and to exercise the unique gifts and calling the Lord has for you at this strategic time in history. If you will do so, great victory lies ahead for the Church of Jesus Christ."35

"Women are allowed to carry and even read from the Bible, but not preach from it; clean and decorate the pulpit but not sit in it; raise money for the church but not participate in the decision of how it is spent or be pretty in the pew rather than intelligent in the Board Room." 36

For sure one of my greatest struggles has been with some of the "sistahs!" As women of God, we have not treated one another with respect or support that we have needed to emerge in the church, government, or society. Satan loves to conquer and divide. He loves to pit the "sistahs" against one another. But it is time for us to become our "sister's keeper." We must have an excellent spirit, be economically free, educated, effective communicators, elegant but modest in our appearance and established in the Word of God. We have many Hurt Ladies that were wounded by the sisters in the church. We need to repent for our pettiness and jealousies of one another. When you reject another sister and pull her down, you are pulling yourself down and you are rejecting yourself. For you see, when I succeed, so do you. When I fall, so do you. We are one Body in Christ.

I am my sister's keeper and much of my spiritual struggle was not so much about me, but it was about the future generations. Somebody had to take the hits and stay in the struggle. My struggles were for my daughter and my spiritual daughters to come. You cannot be your sister's keeper if you are selfish. I never had a natural sister, but I had two brothers. But I have birthed in many spiritual sisters and spiritual daughters during the last twenty years. But they were birthed through "struggle."

We are all in a struggle, but the struggle is not as bad when we are loving on one another. If you are really your sister's keeper, make sure you check yourself from time to time to see if you are really being your sister's keeper and not your sister's "killer" of dreams visions and destiny.

WHEN YOU ARE YOUR SISTER'S KEEPER YOU...

(1) Always speak truth in love to one another

(2) Discern when she is in need or in trouble

(3) Mentor her; don't meddle

(4) Love her unconditionally

(5) Pray and intercede for her

(6) Be quick to forgive and release hurts

(7) Encourage one another; don't compete

(8) Make sacrifices by sowing into her

(9) Don't talk behind her back; cover her back

(10) Rejoice when she overcomes a struggle

Don't be a hater... be your "sister's keeper."

Reflection and Prayer

Check off the areas of your own personal struggle. Take time to pray and reflect on what the Holy Spirit is saying to you in this season. Seek out counsel and deliverance for these areas as needed.

30 -STRUGGLES FOR WOMEN IN MINISTRY

_____1. Lack of assurance of the calling on my life

_____2. Lack of spiritual warfare training

_____3. Ignorance of Satan and his devices

_____4. False allegiances/ ungodly soulties/false burdens

_____5. Have a strong need for acceptance

_____6. Wounded by neglected and restricted interpretations of the Scriptures as it relates to women.

_____7. Denominational and religious control systems that lockdown my calling.

_____8. Sexual harassment

_____9. Experiencing symptoms of rejection that comes from by family and friends and especially by spiritual leadership

_____10. Vulnerable to sexual seduction and sexual compromise

_____11. Fear of Failure

_____12. Rejection by male clergy, women in the congregation and blackballing by pastors and congregations that are taught against women in ministry and not to receive women in pulpit

_____13. Wearing too many hats that drain you of your time and get your misplaced.

_____14. Stepping out of the timing of God.

_____15. Immaturity and running from your calling

_____16. Lack of male and female spiritual mentoring

_____17. Unforgiveness, hurts and bitter roots

_____18. Taking shortcuts to preparation for ministry or little or no preparation

_____19. Lack of a support system as you enter ministry

_____20. Not helping other sisters in the struggle

_____21. Jealous and insecure women in the Body of Christ

_____22. An unsaved or insecure or controlling spouse

_____23. Team ministry with spouse in conflict

_____24. Having trouble balancing singleness or marriage, motherhood, the workplace and ministry

_____25. Struggling with feelings of isolation and loneliness as you relate to the calling of God on your life

_____26. Your spiritual covering is not supportive of your calling or ministry

_____27. Your spiritual covering is pimping your ministry

_____ 28. Wounded spirit and in need of deliverance

_____29. Have received some bad and unsound counsel

_____30. Dealing with betrayals and don't trust anyone

Chapter 14

Hurt and Healed By

The Men in Your Life

"Many women of God are sick in their bodies or miserable, because they will not "drop the issues" against men in their lives that disappointed and wounded them. Some of us need to forgive and release them. Some of us need to go a step further and be reconciled with each other. And still others of us just need to move on and make sure we learned a valuable lesson, that we can pass on to our sons and daughters."
(Bishop Dr. Jackie L. Green)

The Lord began to deal with me about the nine categories of men in our lives that can wound us or protect us: Everyone reading this book can relate to one of these types of men in your life. Maybe you had a father that was your natural in the home or an adopted father, stepfather, foster father, godfather or father-in-law. But also most of us had a grandfather, uncle, brother, boyfriend, husband, male pastor, male boss, supervisor, teach or even dealings with male law enforcement. But there is also the stranger, the man that we might see just passing by but we encounter him through a criminal assault or robbery and maybe a kind gesture. The point I want to make is that the men in our lives shape us and they can either build us up or tear us down. As women in leadership, as wives, mothers, ministers, pastors, teachers and helpmates, God is calling us into a place of real release and forgiveness of those men in our lives that have hurt us.

I thank God for my late grandfather, the Rev. H.B. Matthews who was a real father figure and protector for me. Even though I was a little girl, I wanted to be like him. His strength and covering over my little life was far reaching. But the stepfathers in my life were not so caring or protective. Some of the uncles in my life were "terrorists against girls" and I grew up quickly knowing that male blood relatives could be predators.

One of the most significant pastors in my life was my childhood pastor the late Rev. Dr. W.K. Jackson. He was the closet thing to God and heaven that I could reach out and touch. I had such high respect and regard for him that I believed I could preach too. But I dared not share that dream with anyone because there were no women in the pulpit then. I have had some strong positive male role models in my life, including my own husband. But I have also come to grips with the fact that "men are not the Christ." There is only one Lord and Savior, and he is not a man that He would lie to us.

"We get hurt as women of God because we allow ourselves to worship a man or a ministry, and we put them on a pedestal. We are to blame for idolizing the men in our lives. When those male idols disappoint, betray or wound us, we fall apart. **We need to repent of idolatry of men in our lives.** We have idolized our fathers, pastors, husbands, boyfriends and sons. Idolatry will keep a woman under abuse and domination and in a church or ministry when in fact, she needs to get out . Idolatry keeps many women in a bad marriages, bad   relationships, and under corrupt leadership."

(Bishop Dr. Jackie L. Green)

"It is important for clergy people and other Christians to understand that forgiveness and reconciliation are not one and the same. As stated earlier, forgiveness is a decision on the part of someone who has been wronged to let go and put aside anger, bitterness, hurt, and the desire for retaliation against or punishment of the transgressor. It is a choice that can be made only by the victimized. Reconciliation, on the other hand, is a decision made by both victim and perpetrator(s). It is the restoration of a relationship that has been broken by abuse, betrayal, and other wrongs. Some victims think that if we suggest they consider forgiveness, we're telling them the ought to get back into or reconcile an abusive relationship, ought not to protect themselves, and that the abuse is something that is beyond and gone. But this is not really what forgiveness is. Forgiveness is something that a person grants to another person. It is a gift. Reconciliation is something that's an interpersonal happening. It involves two people, not one. Furthermore, you don't grant reconciliation, you earn reconciliation. Reconciliation is needed when trust has been broken in a relationship." **37**

Every woman has a history and a past that includes encounters with men in their lives. Some times we were wounded. Other times we were protected. According to Thorndike - Barnhart Advanced Dictionary, "help meet" means, "a counterpart; a fit opposite to supply the needs of the former." Why would a husband hurt his helpmate? For sure that man needs to stand before God and even the law or a counselor and give an account. It is true that those that are closest to us can hurt us the most. A woman's husband is closer to her than anyone, and has a place in her heart that no one else can occupy. I have counseled many women who have been hurt by their husbands. Some were hurt indirectly and others directly. These kind of hurts I call "friendly fire." They are fiery darts that come from your team mate. But we must allow the Holy Spirit to provide a way of escape from bitterness, unforgiveness and even spiritual deadness.

I want to talk to those pastor's wives, minister's wives and women in ministry that need healing from broken hearts, betrayal, domestic violence, adultery, and abandonment (physically, emotionally and spiritually) by their mates. It's hard to receive ministry, make love, or be preached to by someone who has hurt you. God meant for our husbands to be our protectors and our healers in many ways. God is calling us as women to deal with the secret or hidden hurts and to tear up our "lists of wrongs" done towards us. There is a "victory place" in ministry that we will not experience until we can "drop the charges." I know, because I used to keep a journal of everything that my husband did that hurt me or disappointed me, until one day God told me to tear it up. When I allowed God to deal with me, then I saw a change coming in him. Many times we are the ones holding up progress. We must allow the Lord to work on us as women of God. If you are an abused women, mentally, physically, economically and even spiritually abused, your deliverance will not be cut and dry. The Holy Spirit will bring our deliverance in layers and little by little. As with natural cuts and bruises, we use a band aid for minor cuts and abrasions. So it is with spiritual injuries. We must not use a band aid on a wound that required stitches or surgery.

Yes, we are called to forgive, but that does not mean we will forget.

"It took me many years to come to the conclusion that forgiveness has nothing to do with forgetting, she said definitively. Instead, it involves giving up the wish to punish or get even with your wrongdoer. I have let go of those thoughts and wishes regarding Bob. But I haven't forgotten all the damage he caused me and our daughter, and I never will. My memories help me measure just how far I've come on my healing journey, she concluded. Remember the past also acts as a early warning system whenever I encounter abusive or violent men."**38**

I think it is important to say to women of God that need to move on in their lives that Jesus Christ our Lord forgave those that crucified Him and betrayed Him at the cross. He said to His Father, "forgive them, for they know not what they do." But Jesus to this day remembers and never forgets the faces of the ones that pierced Him and lied upon Him. I believe one of the reasons Jesus did not forget their faces is because He is at the right hand of the Father interceding for them right now.

WE NEED TO FORGIVE, BUT IT'S NOT ALWAYS A GOOD THING TO FORGET! THERE ARE SOME THINGS WE MUST REMEMBER!

REMEMBER! SO YOU CAN PRAY FOR ALL THE MEN IN YOUR LIFE THAT HURT YOU, AND GIVE THANKS FOR THOSE MEN THAT HELPED YOU.

REMEMBER! SO YOU WON'T MAKE THAT SAME MISTAKE AGAIN!

REMEMBER! SO YOU CAN TELL YOUR DAUGHTERS NOT TO FALL INTO THE SAME TRAPS.

REMEMBER! SO YOU CAN PREACH AND TEACH DELIVERANCE TO ALL THOSE WOMEN WHO NEED TO HEAR YOUR STORY!

REMEMBER! SO YOU WILL BE BETTER PREPARED AND MORE DISCERNING THE NEXT TIME AROUND!

REMEMBER! BECAUSE YOU MIGHT SAVE SOMEONE'S LIFE!

REMEMBER... AND DON'T FORGET HOW GOD

BROUGHT YOU THROUGH! HALLELUJAH!

Our ministries are also suffering because we carry these burdens and weights. There are many Christian pastoral marriages in trouble and in need of biblical counsel. Remember there is great warfare waged against clergy marriages. Don't be naïve. We are in a daily warfare. Also, many pastor's wives need deliverance ministry. They need to have many unclean spirits cast out and broken off of them. Seek out those that can pray for you and set you free of bondages that you have not been able to break.

We must put into practice the scripture that says:

Confess your sins to each other and pray for each other so that you may be healed. The earnest prayer of a righteous person has great power and produces wonderful results. James 5:16 (NLT)

I believe this verse gives us a solution to being healed by our husbands. If we would confess our wrongs to one another and pray for one another, we can begin the process of healing deep hurts. It has taken years and years to deal with my personal issues and the men in my life. But I have crossed over from a land called "Bitter Land" to a to a place called "Better Land." From my book <u>Spurned</u>

into Apostleship, Overcoming Principalities, Powers and People, I preached my own deliverance and hopefully one day you will preach yours too!

"I can preach and declare today,

I'm not bitter, but I'm better

I'm not weaker, but I'm am wiser

I'm not depressed, I am more determined

I'm not down and out, but I'm up and running in His Name

I'm not complaining, but I am celebrating

I'm not broken, but I am beautiful in my season

I'm not wounded, but I am a worshipper, washing my wounds with worship and praise

I'm not angry, but I am apostolic, sent by the Lord

I'm not a hater, but I am a helper, sent to empower the Church

I'm not rejected, but I am accepted and beloved of the Lord

I'm not left behind, but I'm right on time

I'm not living in regret, because God is restoring the years that the enemy has eaten away

I'm not old and wrinkled, but my youth is renewed like the eagle

I'm not ashamed of my journey, but I am anointed by my journey

I'm not ungrateful for my past, because God is upgrading my future

I'm don't feel no ways tired, but I have been tried in the fire

I'm not in bondage anymore, but I am blessed and fancy free like Harriet Tubman; I've doubled back for the captives, so they can walk in that same liberty I'm not fretting or comparing myself to others, but I am highly favored and fruitful in every season I'm not sick and weary in well doing, but I am healed and walking in a new dimension of health I'm not ashamed of my story, cause my story is still in the making, and I'm gonna make sure that God gets all the glory from my story! Hallelujah!" **39**

Take some time now in rest of this chapter and deal with the men in your life past and present.

Twelve Areas of Spousal Hurt

Check those that apply to you.

_____1. Rejection of spiritual gifts and calling on my life

_____2. The Church has become his wife

_____3. Ignores wisdom and prophetic insight I have received

_____4. Adultery(Spiritual and Sexual) (Or spouse on the down low)

_____5. Loss of Intimacy

_____6. Spiritual Decline in my spouse

_____7. Unclean shepherding (falling into sin and neglect)

_____8. Lack of true spiritual covering (opens family to demonic)

_____9. Lack of accountability and integrity

_____10. Abuse (domestic violence)

_____11. Tempted to participate in criminal behavior/imprisonment

_____12. Poor stewardship of wife/children (poor provision and lots of poor decisions)

12 Areas of Spousal Blessing

List twelve ways that your husband has been a blessing to your life. It is important to focus on the POSITIVE and thank the Lord for the blessing that have flowed through our husband.. Write him a love letter today and thank him in a special way. A candle light dinner would be nice too.

1.

2.

3.

4.

5.

6.

7.

8.

9.

10.

11.

12.

Now list seven ways you can show your husband your love and appreciation.

1.

2.

3.

4.

5.

6.

7.

30 WAYS TO BUILD INTIMACY IN MARRIAGE

1. Pray together as a couple

2. Play together

3. Laugh together

4. Sleep together

5. Dine and eat together

6. Procreate together

7. Fast together

8. Worship the Lord together

9. Dance together

10. Exercise together

11. Discipline and raise our children together

12. Vacation and travel together

13. Fellowship with other couples together

14. Make love together

15. Plan and strategize together

16. Save and budget money together

17. Struggle and overcome together

18. Witness for Christ together

19. Walk together

20. Shop and go to movies together

21. Study and read the Bible together

22. Work professionally together

23. Celebrate anniversaries, birthdays and holidays together

24. Study "one another" together

25. Stay together no matter what, in a *Covenant of Love in the Lord*

26. Communicate and celebrate together

27. Dress alike together

28. Serve, sacrifice, suffer and share together

29. Preach and teach together

30. Minister to one another and others together **40**

© 2007 by Pastors Anthony and Dr. Jackie L. Green

Reflection and Prayer

Examine the nine types of men in our lives that can wound us or protect us:

a.   Our Fathers (natural, adopted, step, foster, godfather or inlaw)

b.   Our Grandfathers

c.   Our Uncles

d.   Our Brothers

e.   Our Boyfriends

f.   Our Husbands

g.   Our Pastors (those that were male)

h.   Other Male Authority Figures

   (Boss, supervisors, teachers, law enforcement etc.)

i.   Strangers

An Exercise for Married Women:

I suggest when you have prayed over this section, that you spend time with your husband. Have a special time of consecration where you prepare to wash one another's feet and during the feet washing, confess and repent of hurts and reconcile. After the feet washing anoint, each other's feet with oil and pray. Then spend time loving one another and ministering to one another in an intimate way. Do this from time to time and you will find that healing does take place for the both of you. Share communion together also. This is a way of sealing the healing and what the Lord has done.

An Exercise for All Women:

Reflect upon and address male relationships (from those nine levels) that have hurt you. List them here and be ready to forgive and release them. Ask God what you are to do to bring reconciliation and healing toward them. Then list the names of men in your life that ministered positively to you in some way also.

Men I Need to Forgive and Release	*Men that Have Ministered to Me*
1.	1.
2.	2.
3.	3.
4.	4.
5.	5.
6.	6.
7.	7.
8.	8.
9.	9.
10.	10.
11.	11.
12.	12.

Chapter 15
_____

Hurt Ladies Recovering

Stolen Identities

"The thief's purpose is to steal and kill and destroy. My purpose is to give them a rich and satisfying life." John 10:10 (NLT)

I am amazed as I travel the nation and meet women of God that are "First Ladies" whose identities have been lost, stolen and borrowed by someone or something. The Holy Spirit began to minister to me about the many dimensions of our identities and why Satan begins while we are in our mother's womb to distort and destroy our God given identities. The Bible declares:

"You watched me as I was being formed in utter seclusion, as I was woven together in the dark of the womb. You saw me before I was born. Every day of my life was recorded in your book. Every moment laid out before a single day had passed."

Psalms 139:15-16 (NLT)

In other words, our identity comes from God. I define identity as: "God-given characteristics, gifts, and distinct personality from any other person on the earth which make you an original. Our identity is God's handiwork and handprint on each human life that qualifies them to fulfill their God-given purpose and destiny." Then God began to minister to me about the dimensions of identity. Whenever anyone or anything tampers with our human development with respect to God's plan for us, we experience an identity crisis. We cannot really know our true identity without knowing our Creator. Our identity springs from our Creator.

As women of God, Satan comes to steal our identity, by attacking or corrupting our:

1. Knowledge of our Creator God and knowing we are His creation (Psalms 139:15-16) *We are created in God's image.*

2. Relationship with God our Father, so we won't know we have a purpose and a destiny and a future in Him. (Jeremiah 29:11) *We are a child of God, with a destiny and a future.*

3. Knowledge of birth parents through our natural father and mother (parents) who help to establish our identity. We need to *understand and know about our maternal and paternal inheritance and be able to find identity in both parents.*

4. Knowledge of ancestry/family tribe, family relationship issues and generational bloodline curses or generational blessings. *We all belong to a family and we have roots and identity in the*

family tree.

5. Environments, so that our innocence is destroyed very young by stripping our self- worth and self-esteem by those in authority over us. *We can overcome our negative circumstances and environments.*

6. Childhood and making us grow up too soon and miss significant child development stages necessary for maturity. *Some of us never got to be a little girl, that played and had a childhood because we had so many adult responsibilities put upon us.*

7. Sexuality through incest, molestation, or rape causing sexual confusion and trauma. *Our identity became twisted when we were violated again and again.*

8. Emotional development and balance of my feelings and passions. *We must learn to control and balance our feelings and passions.*

9. Imagination and dreams and making us take on alternative hopes and dreams not our own. *The enemy tries to steal our dreams and distort our imaginations.*

10. Mental health development is dealing with intellect and rational thought patterns. *So a person thinketh, so he is.*

11. Self image is the formation and estimation of my true self. *We learn not to be selfish but considerate of others in the world as*

well as the worth of our own being.

12. <u>Educational and training opportunities</u> needed to equip ourselves and further discover our giftings and abilities. No one should have to *give up their educational goals and desires and settle for less or second best.*

13. <u>Salvation and spiritual</u> understanding of my spiritual man and redemptive purpose.

Those who waste time on carnal and fleshy desires will be spiritual bankrupt.

14. <u>Relationships with men</u> to deceive us and take on the identity that they give us or become invisible in order to survive. *When a woman is hurt by so many men she finds herself unfulfilled in relationships and looking for love in all the wrong places.*

15. <u>Married life</u> and it's purpose for procreation, pleasure and family boundaries. Marriage relationships can rape our identity through poor or desperate decisions, through being soul tied to men that are needy and neurotic and through self neglect on many levels in marriage. Many women think *marriage will give them an identity, but instead it complicate issues and marriage became a dream thief and identity thief occurred.*

16. <u>Physical bodies</u> and physical appearance are important to

our identity. We must understand our bodies as women and take care of our physical bodies. We must not reject ourselves but appreciate how God has formed us as women and not compare ourselves to other women. We must listen to our bodies and not reject our bodies.

Many women spend their whole life rejecting their bodies and their looks. This makes it difficult to find true identity but it also causes women to waste precious years when they could have preserved themselves better.

17. Economic pressures to cripple our finances with long term debts and strangle our real financial capabilities in business and self employment. *Ignorance and poor planning n finances and carrying leeches along the way strip us of economic security.*

18. Moral and Christian values by tempting us to compromise and disobey the Word of the Lord. *When we became disenchanted with religion and church, we find other alternatives to seeking God and truth..*

19. My world view is formed by living in the world around me and discerning world events and its effect on generations.. *"We must be global minded and not self centered to understand our identity."*

20. My voice is evidence of my power to exist and speak. Silencing our voices, making us nameless and faceless women

strips one of all levels of empowerment and spiritual strength to be free to be who God created us to be. *Many women want their voices back, for they soon realize that their voice is connected to empowerment and her identity.*

21. <u>Pleasure and fun</u> is an important part of enjoying life and bringing balance to all the other areas of my life. *Too much pleasure and fun or lack of it can warp one's identity.*

22. <u>My eternal view of life</u> after death is crucial to how I will live my life and how my identity is formed. I realize I am also spirit and will spend eternity somewhere.

For what does it profit me to gain the whole world and lose my soul?

Identity Developmental Chart

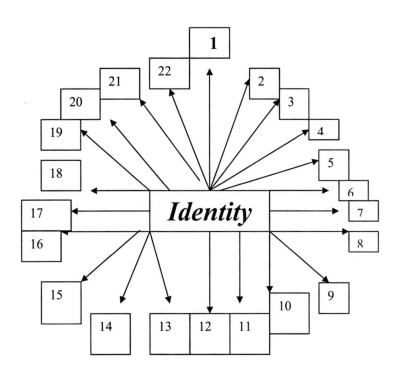

HOW IS OUR IDENTITY FORMED?

1. Creator God	8. Emotions	15. Marriage 22. Eternal View
2. Father God	9. Imagination	16. Physical
3. Parents	10. Mind	17. Economics
4. Family/Tribe	11. Self Image	18. Moral Values
5. Environment	12. Education	19. World View
6. Childhood	13. Spiritual/Soul	20. Our Voice
7. Sexuality	14. Relationships	21. Pleasure/fun

The Lord Jesus Christ has the key to unlock our true identity. He is the only one that can restore a stolen identity. Jeremiah 29:11

When Satan attacks, steals or destroys any portion of our developmental areas of identity, it causes an identity crisis. John 10:10

12 Steps to Recovering Your Spiritual Identity

1. Repent to the Lord and thank Him for your identity.

2. Renounce all rebellion and Satan's hold on your identity.

3. Remove those false identities and put on the true one,

4. Redeem the time by pursuing your true identity.

5. Remember the identity God put in your heart as a little girl.

6. Recall and record the dreams and visions for your identity.

7. Readily accept God's calling in your identity.

8. Release all those persons that hurt you and robbed you of your true identity.

9. Reach forward and don't look back at your past identities.

10. Rest and be refreshed as you walk in your true identity.

11. Release yourself from ungodly vows you made about your identity.

12. Rejoice that God is able to restore and preserve your true identity!

Reflection and Prayer and Discussion

1. Are you a Hurt Lady that is still struggling with who God made you to be and there are principalities, powers and people that stand in the way of your true identity?

2. Are you a Hurt Lady that is running from God and refuse to accept your spiritual identity? Do you lack personal peace because you have not accepted nor received the ministry the Lord has for you?

3. Are you a Hurt Lady who thinks it's too late to pick up your spiritual identity? Is the enemy telling you that you have wasted too much time, or you are too old, or you don't have the strength to birth it forth?

4. Check off the items below that have stripped you of your identity as a woman of God.

_____ My Father	___ Denominationalism	_____School teachers
_____ My Mother	____ Racism	_____My Siblings

_____ Religion and Tradition	____ Abuse/violated	_____Unwed Mother
_____Poverty/Lack	____ Incarceration	_____Sex
_____Traumatic experiences	_____Infirmity/chronic illness	_____Injustices
_____Relationships with men	____Divorce	_____Mental Illness

_____Marriage   _____Rejection   _____Church hurts

_____handicaps   _____Learning disabilities _____Addictions

_____Financial Debts _____Self Hatred   _____Brainwashing

_____Prince Charming _____Husband   _____Pastor

_____Prostitution   _____Prejudice   _____Uneducated

_____Depression   _____Criminal behavior   _____Transient

Chapter 16

Spiritual Mentors

A Remedy for Hurt Ladies

"Oh, my dear children! I feel as if I'm going through labor pains for you again, and they will continue until Christ is fully developed in your lives."
Galatians 4:19 (NLT)

"For even if you have ten thousand others to teach you about Christ, you have only one spiritual father. For I became your father in Christ Jesus when I preached the good News to you. So I urge you to imitate me.

I Corinthians 4:15-16 (NLT)

Those that are called to be mentors or spiritual parents usually have a wealth of knowledge and experience to help the next generation reach their full potential. You will have to shed many tears for your spiritual sons and daughters, as well as precious hours to help launch them into destiny. This is how true sons and daughters are birthed into the earth realm.

There are at least four levels of mentoring that are available to us.

Level 1 (At Personal Times) [42]

Level one is the deepest level where mentoring affects us. This level is usually parents, grandparents, husbands, wives or spiritual confidants. It is early in childhood that we are molded as well as wounded by those having charge over us. These mentors are very important in our spiritual formation because they have access to the vulnerable and very personal areas of our lives. They are foundational mentors/midwives. This level of mentoring can also bring with it generational problems and unhealthy soul ties. This level of mentoring is usually the "entry point" of spiritual blessings as well as generational strongholds.

Level 2 (At Seasonal Times)

I know that there are times when God will bring mentor/midwives for a season. A season represents a term, a period, a duration of time that God wants to accomplish a certain purpose in your life. Seasonal mentoring is helpful in building character. Every mentor has an impartation for our lives. We need to be sensitive to the season we are in and make sure we get all we are to receive. You can't go back and try and retrieve a season. It is a time to receive a deep impartation in the context of a close and personal relationship. Again this seasonal level usually includes being under a pastor, teacher, seminary training or a job related position.

Level 3 (At Kairos Times)

Some mentors/midwives will only be in your life at appointed or kairos times ordained by God. It could be a conference, convention or special event where you sit under their anointing. It seems that just when I have a spiritual deficiency in my life, God will arrange a kairos time for me to receive from a spiritual mentor. The appointed times are usually "very intense." The appointed times are "life changing." Kairos times usually come when we have other plans. Kairos times usually require great sacrifice from our regular schedules. It is important to pay attention to God when He is saying, "pick up and go" to a certain place to receive "fresh manna." One kairos moment can be so important and intense that it is equal to getting two or three years of training in one day's time from that mentor.

Level 4 (From a Distance)

Sometimes persons at a distance must mentor us because they live in another city or nation. From a distance you can be mentored through their books, tapes and videos. Every book or tape they author must be in your personal library. There is an impartation from their lives as you read and study their materials. I had to learn this very early in my spiritual growth or I would have dried up and died. Some of my mentors were across the nation and I could not afford to fly in and chat with them. But God has a way to import the wisdom and knowledge we need through the mentor's resources.

A spiritual father or spiritual mother can help heal the hurts because:

- They have the love of the Father working in them. They are patient and tolerant of where you are. They have a love for future generations. They will not be jealous of you and won't strip or uncover you, but cover you in your times of hurt and weakness.

- They walk in high godly character and that means you can follow in their holy example or footsteps.

- They walk in truth and transparency. They are honest and open with you and will call you back to righteousness and accountability.

- They have something spiritual and wise to impart (to pass on to you) because they have been proven.

- They are willing to travail, teach, and labor with you while they are steadily pouring into your life.

- They are there to build a relationship, while you may have come out of a season of loneliness and bad relationships. They are willing to spend time with you and walk you through a healing process.

- Their major desire for you is that Christ be formed in you and that the glory of the Lord would shine forth in your life, and outshine the hurt and disappointments in ministry.

- They won't use you or abuse you. They can see your pain and they are sensitive enough to pull out your true potential.

- They can see the blockages and they become a bridge for you.

- They can see others have pimped you, but they invest in you.

- They see your frustration so they lay new foundations.

- They see your wounds, and they can teach you how to wash those wounds with worship and rebuild from the ashes.

- They discern something is missing and they can usually impart the missing links.

- They see your fears and they can speak courage into your future.

- They see your rejection so they release love and acceptance.

- They see you've been a misfit, but help you discover your true identity, and become fitly joined in the Body of Christ.

FIRST AID

Reflections and Prayers

Ask God to send spirituals mentors into your life to help bring about healing and wholeness. List the names of spiritual mentors that God has already given to you already. Spend some time giving thanks for them and even sow a seed of kindness and appreciation back into them as the Lord leads you.

Chapter 17

Healed from Two Types of Widowhood

"Fear not, you will no longer live in shame. Don't be afraid; there is no more disgrace for you. You will no longer remember the shame of your youth and the sorrows of widowhood. For the Creator will be your husband; the Lord of Heaven's Armies is his name! He is your Redeemer, the Holy One of Israel, the God of all the earth. For the Lord has called you back from your grief, as though you were a young wife abandoned by her husband," says your God. "For a brief moment I abandoned you, but with great compassion I will take you back." Isaiah 54:4-7 (NLT)

God has a special place in His heart for widows and orphans. He is their protector and provider when they have been abandoned and left without spiritual and natural covering. I have always had a heart for widows that were pastor's and minister's wives. Many times they are left alone, uncovered, and uncared for by the church once their husbands are gone. Many of those widows never got the healing and deliverance they needed before they became a widow. They no longer had a voice once their husbands were dead. They had many unresolved issues, and many had experienced injustices. Unless God vindicates them, they will not receive justice.

I also want to acknowledge those women whose husbands are alive but they are "spiritual widows." In other words, their husbands are on a whole different spiritual level, lagging behind in spiritual things, which has left them spiritually separated and left her spiritually alone in her journey at important spiritual elevations in her life. Many pastor's wife have walked a lonely road not being spiritually yoked together with their husbands. You have been a *spiritual widow* whose heart has ached to share deep spiritual truths with him, but he would not receive it. You have grieved for him, and you have prayed for him, but he has not wanted to come up into deep things of God, nor could he bring the people of God under his leadership to that deep place in God. You have walked in a rich place, while he was content to stay in a barren place, but it was lonely place for you. For though you appear to be in the same room, you are not in the same room spiritually. That is spiritual widowhood, but God has a word for you too. He is the only one that can heal your heart in the natural and spiritual of widowhood. I felt a release of a prophetic word to widows whose husbands were pastors and gave their lives and livelihood for the ministry.

PROPHETIC WORD TO THE WIDOWS...
FROM BISHOP Dr. Jackie L. Green- June 15, 2008

The Lord says:

"For I have a special place in My heart for the widow and the orphan. For both have been abandoned and both are devalued by society even in My Church. I have seen your tears, loneliness and poverty too. I have heard your heart cry for justice, where there was no justice. And I shall heal thee with My Word. I shall speak a Word to thy spirit and cause thy spiritual womb to leap once again. And I shall bring peace to thee and I shall vindicate thee from church hurts and church abuse. And you shall cry and weep no more. You shall no longer mourn because of church politics and church bureaucracy. For I am allowing my Spirit to fall upon you afresh, and my sons and daughters, my widows and orphans, my handmaidens shall find new and fresh meaning in serving Me.

And I shall cause old hurts to be healed; and I shall raise up my spiritual and natural widows in the last days to be fruitful and multiply their wisdom and compassion to many. For I need thee says God. I need the widows to arise, and like the widow of Zarephath, I need you to minister to the Elijahs and Elishas of your day. I need you to speak into the Deborahs and the Esthers of your day. I need

243

you like the widow Anna, to find your place of intercession and prayer in the Temple, and make a difference in the next generation. And I call thee to bless the babies and bless the unborn babies too. For there is much work in your times of widowhood. No time to mourn. But it is time to dance. You have cried and wept enough, so laugh now at the enemy. No time to hate those that hurt you, but bless your enemies. No time to stay in the past, but it is time to put your past behind you, and use it as a stepping stone to the future. I call thee forth out of your grave clothes and cause you to put your black veils away, and let your fruitful days arise.

For I have not forgotten you, O widow of mine. O pastor's wife, I have not forgotten you. O pioneering women, forgive and remember not the former things, and arise and be strong says God. For this is your time; this is your hour; and I shall be a husband to you, and a covering for thee this hour," says the Spirit of the Living God.

And to the spiritual widow, I will use you daughter, in spite of what feels like spiritual widowhood in the Spirit. And you shall remain fruitful, faithful and with a fresh pair of eyes. Your reward is great because you have obeyed and you have hungered for truth at it's highest level. I will fill the voids and I will continue to woo him to

244

bring him up into the high places says God, and cause you both to set your faces like flint for the deeper things of Me. For I will not hold you responsible for the choices that he makes and I will not allow thee to be ashamed. But I will cover thee with my feathers in the secret place of the Most high, says the Spirit of the Lord."

Reflections and Prayer

List the names of pastor's wives and minister's wives and women in ministry that are widows. Spend time in prayer for them today and any time the Holy Spirit prompts you to pray for them. List the names of those widows here that God is calling you to pray for. Many widows are hurting as former pastor's wives and women in ministry are serving God and are still widows. What is God saying you are to do to minister to the hurts in their lives?

Chapter 18

Steps to Deliverance and Healing

"And all of this is a gift from God, who reconciled us back to himself by Jesus Christ, and has given to us the ministry of reconciliation."

I Corinthians 5:18

This chapter is very key to the healing that is so needed for preacher's wives and women in ministry. I want to examine the reasons we get hurt and how to guard our hearts in the future from these hurts. God said, "Jackie I want you to toughen up as you weather church hurts and trials of life, but never allow your "heart" to become "hard" and never stop "loving and believing in people." A soft heart will always keep you open and teachable, merciful and forgiving, and able to still see the good in people, as well as love your enemies. A soft heart manufacturers God's love and grace. KEEP YOUR HEART SOFT. I know God meant for our homes, churches and schools to be "safe places" to nurture us, not abuse or hurt us. We must heal the church hurts so that we can become God's healing agents to a hurting world. How do we end up as Hurt Ladies?

14 Reasons We Become Hurt Ladies

- There are layers of personal and childhood baggage she needs to deal with
- She tries and fails to meet the expectations that the church puts on her
- She tries and fails to meet the expectations her spouse puts on her
- Not spiritually mature and still on the milk of the Word and not meat
- Has no one she can trust or confide in (especially a mentor)
- She doesn't know who she is in Christ or her purpose and calling
- Ignorance of spiritual warfare
- Expecting the Church to be a perfect place instead of a hospital for the sick
- Betrayal from those she trusted inside and outside the church
- Uncovered and not highly valued by her spouse
- Tries to cover and fill in for spouse's shortcomings
- Does not know or discern the Voice of the Lord with clarity

in her life

- She is a buffer for her husband and children and gets caught in the crossfire
- Not valuing herself and her own personal and spiritual development
-

17 Steps to Recovery From Church Hurts

- Admit that you have been hurt and need to be healed of the church abuse or church hurts
- Forgive and release everyone that has hurt or abused you
- Turn to God and give Him back your total trust
  Repent for looking to the church as the "Savior" and remember they are human beings like you
- Repent and take ownership for your own sins and spiritual blindness in the situation
- Release all offenses, anger, bitterness and false expectations to God
- Take time out to fast and pray for direction: Should I shift positions?
- Seek counseling from someone that you can trust in the situation
- What does the Word of God say about this situation? Find

scripture.

- Give yourself time to heal and recover

- Don't poison others about the church because you got hurt

- How does this hurting experience help you to grow and go to the next level?

- Repent for not listening to the warnings of the Holy Spirit

- Check yourself to make sure you have been born again and are filled with the Holy Spirit

- Get deliverance ministry for those deep layers of hurt and abuse by submitting to a deliverance ministry team/church and get those areas cleansed.

- Learn from your mistakes and from this painful situation and seek to strengthen others by what you have learned

- Sit down and journal your desires and reasons for being in your church and see if your purpose in Christ is being fulfilled. If you must leave a church, resign from some positions and get refocused, seek the Lord first, share it with your spouse, then make your decision. Sometimes, we just need a selah and other times we need a complete change.

Reflections and Prayer

What is the Holy Spirit saying to you at this time about your personal church hurts and even hurts in your singleness, or marriage and ministry? Journal your thoughts here. What areas are you at fault and need to take ownership?

Chapter 19

What the Church Owes

Every Hurt Lady

"I pray that they will all be one, just as you and I are one, as you are in me, Father, and I am in you. And may they be in us so that the world will believe you sent me."(NLT)

The very thing the church owes to those that are hurting is the very thing Jesus prayed for in John 17:21. The world is watching the Church on worldwide television and every Sunday morning in local parishes. They are watching how we treat one another and how we live our daily lives. They are watching tele-evangelists and every money scandal, divorce and pulpit domestic violence. Non-believers are not convinced that Jesus is Lord and was sent by God because we have so much hurt, pain and division among believers. When the church takes ownership for her behavior and starts to reconcile with one another, and the world sees unity on every level, they will surely believe Jesus is Lord.

"Equality is not a privilege to be earned by women, but a right

which belongs to them by virtue of their creation in the image
of God. Equality leads to acceptance, respect, sharing mutuality,
appreciation, friendship and partnership; inequality to domination,
superiority, disrespect, lack of appreciation, de-valuing, and
stereotyping, in a word, to sexism."**43**

What Christ wants most for the church is "unity and oneness"
in Him. *The Body of Christ cannot continue to hurt and reject one*
another. The Church can help to fulfill the prayer of our Lord for
unity by treating the First Lady, the pastor's wife, the minister's wife,
the woman in ministry, the female pastor and women and girls in
the Body with an equality and respect that Christ has already given
to them. This reconciliation and healing is not just from men in the
Body of Christ, but it is also needed by women who have also been
enemies of the First Lady and women in leadership. Some of my
deeps wounds came from jealous women and women haters in the
Body of Christ. There is much reconciliation and unity that must
begin among women in the church. I have tried to make the steps to
reconciliation and healing simple. Whether you are male or female,
you must begin to reconcile your differences and repent for your part
in hurting a pastor's wife, minister's wife, women preachers or women
in leadership roles. You can begin with an:

1. **Apology** - Another word for apology is "atonement" which means repentance. Take the time and sincerely apologize to those women of God that you have hurt and disrespected. Repent and confess your sins against her. Ask for her forgiveness. Apologize so that the next generation can see it and be healed as well. A sincere apology goes a long way and can prevent generations from being perverted.

2. **Appreciation** - Obey the leading of the Holy Spirit and show your love and appreciation by kind acts and making personal sacrifices for the First Lady and the pastoral family. When you bless her, you bless the pastor. Take time to say thank you and don't just do it during the Pastor's Anniversary. If your senior pastor is a woman, then why not show appreciation to the "First Man, her husband?"

3. **Awareness** - Don't ignore the injustices and harsh treatment toward the Hurt Lady by your "silence." Make others aware and take steps toward dealing with the pain. The sin of omission is great where we have to take risk and stand up for what is right. The Church must take ownership for the many "Hurt Ladies" in the church today.

4. **Alignment** - This means that the Church needs to make sure that everyone is given the opportunity to be in spiritual alignment and fitly joined in the Body of Christ regardless of denomination or traditions. Alignment has nothing to do with gender but according to the purpose and plan of God on our lives. The Church cannot come into their divine purpose and alignment until women are given their rightful place as partners and joint heirs. Women of God must be allowed to find and flow in their spiritual gifts and callings.

5. **Acceptance** - This means that it's time for the Church to accept the fact that God created male and female to walk together as a team in the earth and that the work of evangelism cannot be accomplished in the earth with just men. God has created them as equal partners to get the job done. The Church must stop excluding and oppressing women, and begin to include them and bless them. They must be accepted as the beloved of the Lord.

6. **Affirmation** -This means the church needs to applaud what God is already doing through women. The church needs to come into agreement with the plan of God on her life that was set in motion before the foundation of the earth was laid.

The church is basically saying "yes and amen".

7. **Asylum** - This means protection and safety. First Ladies, women in ministry, and yes all the Daughters of Zion need to feel that the church is a safe ground and not a battle ground. The church must no longer be a battle zone but an asylum, sanctuary, a safe place to find peace, rest, protection and a fortress from the enemy. It should especially be a place of asylum for the battered and abused woman.

I believe in reconciliation and healing for pastoral families and the congregations that we serve. Thank God we now have a greater revelation than we did even 20 or 30 years ago on spiritual warfare and how to defeat the enemy. *Hurt Ladies* all over the world are coming into divine alignment and are being affirmed of their God given place in the Body of Christ. Pastor's wives are taking on new roles in team ministry by serving with their husbands. The preacher's children (PK's) are a growing part of the family ministry team and not a casualty. We must prophesy and speak forth the mind of God for "generation now and generation next." We must prepare them to be able to accept the mantles that are being passed to them. They are the "new generation" and a "new breed."

FIRST AID

Prayer and Reflection

List the names of all the churches or ministries you have served in. Begin to release them of any hurts, neglect, bondages, religious abuse, wounds and trauma they may caused you knowingly and unknowingly. This includes the pastor, leaders, and church-at-large. Release a blessing back to them and trust God to heal you and protect others from them in the future. If there were sexual abuse, molestation, rape and other crimes against you, you need to get counseling immediately and also consider pressing charges for these violations. This will protect other women and young girls and even boys from those same violations. Remember domestic violence and sexual assault is a sin, a crime and a learned behavior.

Chapter 20

A Word to God's Daughters

(From Bishop Dr. Jackie L. Green)
November 4, 2008
(Presidential Election Day)

"Mordecai sent this reply to Esther. "Don't think for a moment that because you're in the palace you will escape when all other Jews are killed. If you keep quiet at a time like this, deliverance and relief for the Jews will arise from some other place, but you and your relatives will die. Who knows if perhaps you were made queen for just such a time as this? Then Esther sent this reply to Mordecai: Go and gather together all the Jews of Susa and fast for me. Do not eat or drink for three days, night or day. My maids and I will do the same. And then, though it is against the law, I will go in to see the king. If I must die, I must die. So Mordecai went away and did everything as Esther had ordered him."
Esther 4:13-17 (NLT)

I hear the Spirit of the Lord say in the 21st Century, I am calling for the Esthers of your day to arise and not love their comforts or conveniences more than the cry of My people, but turn their plates down and fast like Esther, and be willing to give up all for the next generations of My people. I am raising up a new breed of women servants, who will not buckle under rejection and religious warfare.

But you are the daughters that your mothers cried out to Me about.
And I have removed many of the obstacles that your foremothers
encountered. But I have left some obstacles for thee to overcome,
or you might become prideful and haughty. Now you must run
a swifter and smarter race with discernment and a new level of
dedication says God. It has taken almost 2000 years for the Church
to get a vision of the gift in you, the Daughters of King, called to
bring balance to the male counterpart and to the Church. For such
a time as this, like as with Esther, I have caused many daughters to
go before you and pave the way for thee to be all that I created you
to be. There have been many women in the pulpits and the pews
that were scarred by religion and the traditions of men, as they were
trying to evolve and fulfill their God given destiny and purpose. But
I say to you *daughters of the King*; it is your time. I say to you *women
that publish the Word*; it is your season. I say to you that are *daughters
of circumstance*, that have hit rock bottom; this is your time to get
up and run your race that has been set before you. I say to those
women that are aged and seasoned like honey wine, and in their golden
years too, lay your hands on yourself and the young and strengthen
both, for you still have much work to do. And even as you have
seen the tip of reconciliation in America with the election of Senator
Barak Obama as the new President of the United States, it took over
200 years to see integration on the top level of government. And

so it will be with my *daughters of destiny,* that have struggled in the church houses of America, to be valued and received by other parts of the Body of Christ. In this next lap, I am raising up Daughters that will be wise as serpents but harmless as doves. They will not be intimidated and crave to be accepted by the status quo. But they are the daughters birthed out of the afflictions of their mothers. They are the daughters that shall not be ashamed of their Mother Eve, but shall declare and decree they are the equal partner to Adam in this day, and they shall arise and be Kingdom bulldozers and builders. Today in many nations of the world, women and girls do not have the opportunities that women have in America. *And I shall begin to allow a fresh fountain and stream to flow out of this nation through my Healed Ladies, for you cannot go to the nations as Hurt Ladies. I am about to deploy a group of women to the nations that are tough, tried and true and can stand against the powers of darkness in the global community but tender in heart like Me.*

I call you *"Now women"* this hour." I am calling women with a sense of urgency, that will not buckle under the pressures of warfare, but will pray now, prepare now, shift now, move forward now, take a risk now, serve now, preach now, teach now, disciple others now, conceive the Promises now, birth in the next move of God now, commit now, get stirred up now, push through to your victory now, fly anywhere for the Kingdom now, praise and worship Me now, forgive now, sacrifice now, have faith now, believe Me now, get delivered now, and trust and obey Me now! Wash your wounds with worship now! *It is the "NOW LADY" that I am calling forth to impact the future generations of women leaders!* For the cemetery is full of **Hurt Ladies** who can't do what they need to do NOW! But you have time now! I am calling for the "Now" Woman…not the "Later Woman". You are not the ones I need this hour if you have excuses and exemptions from suffering and separation for the sake of the Gospel. I am releasing upon thee even in this prophetic Word this hour, a great desire to birth in the nations of the world and be whole while you are doing it. Your spiritual mothers are arising on your behalf, for many of them have been too wounded to travail or transition on your behalf. But the time has also come for many of you to arise and birth sons and daughters in the Spirit and to mentor them. And there shall be a triple fold release of women pastors, women ministers, pastoral ministry teams with strong husband and wives walking together because of this very book, your young teen daughters and young adult women shall arise quicker, than their mothers did, to preach, prophesy, pray and proclaim the Gospel to the nations! This is the hour. This is the Word of the Lord to My Daughters of Deborah and Esther too. Touch and agree with your spiritual mothers and with your natural mothers and with your grandmothers, for many of them were the praying matriarchs that sustained great warfare for you to stand up this hour. Touch and agree with your sisters-in-ministry and cheer one another on to the next place that awaits thee. Touch and agree with the brethren, your brothers in Christ and those in the ministry, and gird them up and help them, for I have anointed you to be a helpmate, and you both need one another to fulfill the Great Commission. And because so many of My daughters have said "I don't want to be like my mother," the Lord says you were letting your hurts and wounds talk. And though you shall not be clones of your mothers, I created you to resemble her in those godly ways and I have called you daughters to supercede what your mothers did and you shall do greater works and exploits because of her prayers. But never forget from whence you have come My daughters, for you were launched on the tears and years of sacrifice of your mothers. Now this is the hour. This is your time. Take your place now Esther and Elizabeth, Deborah and Dorcas, Sarah and Salome, Ruth and Rahab , Abigail and Anna, Mary and Martha, Lydia and Lois, Tamar and Dinah, and run with the baton that is being passed to **you for such a time as this**, from your spiritual mothers, mentors and midwives, and your Master, says the Spirit of the Living God!

Bishop Dr. Jackie Green and her daughter Elyzabeth Green standing together today as family, friends and partners in ministry.

Chapter 21

Hurt Ladies With The Power to Bless

Hurt Ladies of the Lord will know that their healing has begun to spring forth when they are able to bless those that have wounded them and hurt them. This is a true sign that your deliverance has come. There are seven ways to be a blessing to others and we find them in the scriptures below. This is a key for *Hurt Ladies* being *"Healed Ladies."* **To bless means to speak well of, to praise, or to call down God's gracious power; also to guard and protect, or to ask God's favor upon; or, to mark with blood.**

It is important before we end our journey together in this book that we understand the power of blessing others is greater than the power to curse others. These principles will change your life as you put them into practice and become a **"Blessed Lady that is a Blessing."** There are valuable lessons to learn from these seven Bible characters whose lives were transformed and the lives of others were transformed by them. We must know and discern when to use our power to bless others.

1. Widow of Zarepheth - I Kings 17:8-24

I will use my power to bless others in my time of famine, desperation and in times of great need. I have fed many at my table who have hurt me and betrayed me, but I blessed them anyway. I was able to extend hospitality even though they did not deserve it. I knew that God was using me to be a blessing and in my obedience I was healed sometimes emotionally and sometimes physically. The widow of Zarepheth became a blessing to the Prophet Elijah during the time of famine and during the time she was preparing to die herself. Because she put the prophet of the Lord before the needs of herself and her son, a prophetic word was released to her that there would always be "flour and olive oil left in her containers as a promise from the Lord. The widow did not know that some time later her son would get sick and die. But Elijah went before the Lord on her behalf and cried out because this woman had blessed him in times past. The Lord heard Elijah's prayer and the life of the child returned. **I am convinced that because my husband and I blessed so many others in our home by feeding and housing them, our children have never lacked when they went away to college.** They always had someone open their homes to them and feed them. Our ability to bless others will also bless our seed in ways we least expect. The son of the widow woman reaped the blessing of new life and resurrection because his mother used her power to bless the prophet of the Lord.

2. Abraham – Genesis 14:17-20

I must find and use my power to bless my Melchizedek in my life. These are people who unlock my destiny; who father or mother me, open provision to me, provide accountability and protection for me, and are greater in the Spirit than I. This is very important for women in ministry because you must find ways to bless and pour into those that have been a blessing to us. Abraham gave a tenth to the High Priest of Salem named Melchizedek. But before he did that, Melchizedek gave Abram bread and wine. He sowed first. I believe this bread and wine spiritually represented what spiritual parents give to us. The bread is substance, the Word of God, and the wine is the spiritual increase of revelation and insight we gain and the power of the Spirit upon our lives. I believe that this encounter unlocked revelation in Abraham's life and signaled a move of God. True mentors always move us forward. Abraham was glad to bless Melchizedek. I am amazed at how many spiritual sons and daughters I do have, and how many of them don't remember the "launching pad they came from." Some were never really knitted to my heart and mantle, so they came and went. But those that I have really poured my life into, and they have received it with thanksgiving and respect, they find ways to bless me. It's important to thank those spiritual mothers and fathers who labored with you. From time to time I even let my former pastors and mentors know how I am doing and I bless them unexpectedly. I am thankful for the Melchizedeks in my life and those ministries they represent that have given me bread and wine in my times of great need and desperation.

3. Jacob - Genesis 47:7, 49:1

I will use my power to bless those in authority in the government, the marketplace, and in high ranking positions, when God tells me. This is key even in the blessing of your pastor, your husband and those that have spiritual oversight in your life. Jacob blessed Pharaoh. That really shocked me when I read it. He blessed a pagan ruler. That taught me that we can bless those in government and even those that don't believe in Christ. We never know how that will affect that leader or their seed for generations to come. I have been blessed to be on various prayer assignments with governmental leaders and I always blessed them with something pertaining to the Word of God. Jacob even laid hands I believe on the Pharaoh, because that was the way blessings were imparted in those days, especially when passing the blessing to the next generation. Even a pagan Pharaoh wanted to receive a blessing. I don't have time to be bitter, but I would rather use my power to bless others than to complain and curse others. Americans have been notorious for cursing their President and government. We have the power to bless our nation, and we need to begin with our words. Blessing is more powerful than cursing.

4. Joseph - Genesis 41:37-44

I will use my power to bless others with my spiritual gifts (Word of Wisdom, Word of Knowledge and the Prophetic, and Healing Gifts) and bless others through what I have suffered which will and can affect future generations. Never withhold the operation of your spiritual gifts as a means of being vindictive. The gifts don't belong to us but are for the Body of Christ. Some women get so bitter that they cannot flow in anything, and it's probably best they don't at that time. But be careful that you don't find yourself spewing out "bitter waters" instead of sweetness. Hurts make you bitter and not a sweet smelling incense unto the Lord. Joseph was a dreamer and one with strong prophetic insight and administrative skill. Even while in prison, Joseph's spiritual gifts were blessing those that had him in captivity. There is someone you can bless with your giftings, without always looking to be compensated. God does take care of us and compensate us in ways we never imagined. **I live to be a blessing and therefore I cannot stay hurt or wounded for long. I cannot afford to have "bitter waters" coming out of my life to others.**

5. David- II Sam. 6:17-23

I will use my power to bless others through my worshipping of my God. I will also bless the people of many nations by governing in righteousness and setting a godly example. Keep your worship pure and bless the Lord at all times. This will keep you balanced and keep your heart in the right place. When your worship dries up, you dry up. King David is a prime example of worship transforming his life and everyone around him. David brought transformation to a whole nation through his passionate worship the God of Israel. Our worship can be a blessing because it brings healing and causes tormenting spirits to be harnessed.

David played his harp and blessed King Saul. The evil spirits would subside when the worship music of the Lord was played. Worship is healing not only for others, but it heals us. **Wash your hurts with worship.** I have found a place in the presence of the Lord in my worship that apprehends all my anxiety and cares. Let others see you worship, and it will bless them.

6. Abigail- I Samuel 25:10-13, 18, and verses 32-33

I will use my power to bless because my destiny could be connected to that very act of blessing. My power to bless could save the lives of others. Abigail had wisdom and the power to bless. You can't use your power to bless for foolish gain. But Abigail knew to bless King David because Nabal, her husband had insulted him. Her quick act to bless later opened the door for her to become the wife of the King. She had no idea that her destiny was connected to those she blessed. My power to bless is also a form of intercession and interception. Blessings are stronger than curses. Abigail was some kind of woman. She was married to fool and she was probably a wounded woman. But she didn't let her wounds stop her from being a blessing.

7. JESUS CHRIST OUR LORD- John 3:16 and Luke 23:34

I will use my power to bless because Jesus blessed me and looked beyond my faults and saw my needs. There are numerous examples in the New Testament of lives that were changed because our Lord looked beyond their faults and saw the need. Jesus "so loved the world," and that was His motivation for blessings others. From the life of our Lord Jesus Christ we learn to:

1. Bless the Lord at all times

2. Bless with a loving touch or loving glance

3. Bless with a kind word or encouragement

4. Bless others through our overflow and through sacrifice

5. Bless others by imparting wisdom and love

6. Bless through spiritual gifts, talents, skills and expertise

7. Bless through money and resources

8. Bless the vision of other ministries

9. Bless those that hurt us especially if it is in our power to do good

10. Bless by planting seeds in good ground

11. Bless our enemies that persecute and despitefully use us

12. Bless others because we are fulfilled and are most like Jesus when we are able to love and bless others, and see their lives changed and transformed.

HERE IS WISDOM:

Don't expect your return from those that you bless.

BLESSING OTHERS WITH A CLEAN HEART

WILL KEEP YOUR GATES OPEN FOR GOD TO WORK

THROUGH ANY DOOR HE CHOOSES TO BLESS

YOU.

FIRST AID

Reflections and Prayer

Think about those that you can bless. Remember the different levels and ways to bless. Make some notes here on those you want to bless, even blessing your enemies. This is evidence of your breakthrough.

Lord, give me seeds and resources so I can be a blessing to the following people, ministries or situations:

Chapter 22

Hurt Lady

Prayer of Declaration

Dear Heavenly Father,

I come before you today and ask that You create in me a clean heart and renew a right spirit within me. I know that I am fearfully and wonderfully made. Keep me in Your perfect will and let my purpose and destiny be established in You. Establish my going out and my coming in. Help me to never forget that You are my Rock. When my heart is overwhelmed, lead me daily to the Rock that is higher than I. In that secret place hide me. I declare that I will dwell in the secret places of the Most High God and there I will linger in Your Presence. Help me to be quiet before You, and to wait upon You. For though my enemies come upon me to eat my flesh and destroy my household and ministry, I will wait quietly before the Lord, for my enemies want me to fall from my set position. But no

matter what, I am going through. I will not be shaken. I declare
that none of these things move me from Your set purposes for me. I
have victory and honor in You, O God. I am a chosen vessel, a royal
priesthood, a holy woman, a godly woman, and I will praise You
with everything that is within me. And like King David, everyday,
I will encourage myself in the Lord. I will be encouraged and not
discouraged. And though the enemy rises up against me and comes
in like a flood, Lord You will lift up a standard against my enemies.
I am convinced that nothing can ever separate me from Your love.
Not even life and death situations, not angels or demons, not worries
about tomorrow, nor the powers of hell can separate me from Your
love and protection. I will bless You at all times and Your praises shall
continually be in my mouth.

Father, forgive my sins and help me to release and forgive all those
who have hurt me or betrayed me. Teach me to love my enemies and
respect what You are doing in my life through my enemies. Teach me
how to love unconditionally and to learn quickly the lessons I need
to learn in times of struggle. Help me to turn my "pain" into gain
for the Kingdom. Because of my pain I will "reign" with You, Lord,
over my enemies. ***Help me to be better and not bitter, and to value
every part of my journey.*** Pull out every bitter root, all resentment,
all rejection and all infirmity that has settled in my heart. Heal me,

O Lord, so that I will not be bound by the enemy. Give me a love for difficult people and those who have hurt me and my family. Teach me not to withhold that which I can do to bless others. Make me a woman that blesses others so I can experience the greater glory.

I pray that my ambitions and my desires are always to please the King, and I seek the Kingdom of God first and His righteousness. I thank you that I am a Kingdom citizen and I am not bound by religion and traditions of men. I have a higher calling and a higher perspective. I will not allow the kingdom of darkness to overtake me, for I sit in heavenly places in Christ Jesus and I am more than a conqueror through Christ Jesus. I am pressed on every side by trials and troubles, but I am not crushed. In times of depression and perplexing situations, I am not driven to despair. Sometimes I feel like the hounds of hell are hunting me down, but I know Father, You will never abandon me. My body suffers from time to time but I know you are the God that healeth me. By Your Blood and by Your stripes You took my diseases. I realize that I must keep my spirit man strong so that my body can fight off any disease and weakness.

Father help me to deal with the things that I cannot change. **Let Your grace be sufficient for me.** I have prayed about many things, and where there has been no change in circumstances yet, there is a constant change in me. Let Your great grace rest upon me for the things that I must endure. Let me not be a complainer or one that murmurs. Let my words be few and seasoned with life and liberty. Let me not be contaminated by my own words or the negative words of others. Let my faith be built up as I pray in the Holy Spirit, building up my spirit man daily.

I thank You that I have the revelation that there is no longer Jew or Gentile, slave or free, male and female, for we all are ONE in Christ Jesus. Let me be a voice for You, Lord, to preach truth and liberty. I declare and decree that the Spirit of the Lord is upon me and I am anointed to bring Good News to the poor. I have been sent to bind up the broken hearted and to proclaim that captives will be released and prisoners will be freed. I am sent to tell those that mourn that the time of the Lord's favor has come and with it has come God's anger against His enemies. I thank You Father that You will use me to rebuild the ancient ruins and repair churches, cities and nations. I am a priest of the Lord, and a minister of God. Thank you that I am coming into a season where instead of shame and dishonor, I shall begin to enjoy life and enjoy a double share of honor. I thank you for my double portion of prosperity and everlasting joy which is mine. Father, You love justice and I love justice too.

Lord I further declare that I am blessed in the city and in the field. My marriage is blessed and my children are blessed to many generations. My children will be successful everywhere they go. Our household shall have more than enough and we shall always keep our home open to those in need. We are the lenders and not the borrowers. We will conduct our business affairs rightly. We will overcome evil with good. I decree that God is the only One that can minister vengeance, **so I give up my right to "get even,"** and I will allow God to execute justice. Father, help me to never turn away from You or be angry with You, but I will keep your commandments and trust in You with all my heart and lean not to my own understanding. I thank You that I am a cheerful giver and faithful tither and I know You have rebuked the devourer for my sake. I thank You that you are restoring the years that the cankerworm has tried to eat away at my prosperity and blessings.

I thank You that as a wife or one that will become a wife some day, that I will be a woman that can wear many hats and be balanced and have my priorities in order. I thank You for Deborah who showed us how to be a woman of many hats. Let me be a woman, a wife (in due season) and mother (or spiritual mother) to many, a prophetic woman with insight, a judge, one that loves righteousness and treats others fairly, a military strategist, which is one that knows

how to execute spiritual warfare and yes, I am a true worshipper. I
know You look for women that will worship You in Spirit and in
truth. For I love to worship You and dance before You and tell
others of Your wondrous works.

Lord, teach my hands to war and my fingers to fight. I will put
on the whole armor of God so that I will be able to stand against
the wiles of the Devil. I will not use carnal weapons, but spiritual
weapons to outsmart the enemy. I thank You for teaching me how
to appropriate the Blood, your Name, the Word and use my spiritual
discernment. I take authority over all witchcraft and root workings
and divination that has been sent and worked against me, my home,
and the ministry. I break the power of all evil altars, and declare that
the Blood of Jesus is all powerful and that the Word of God is sharper
than any two edged sword against the enemy. I release the fire of
the Lord against demonic forces and ask that the angels be released
to encamp around me and do battle for me. I decree and declare
that there is a strong protective hedge around me and my household
and ministry, and I am secure and safe from all forms destruction.
I decree and declare that no weapon formed against my household
shall prosper and every tongue that shall rise up against us, we shall
condemn, for this the heritage of the saints of the Lord. I take
spiritual authority over every plot and evil conspiracy to ambush the

plans of God for my life, family and ministry. Daily I overcome the enemy by the Blood of the Lamb, by the Word of my testimony and I love not my own life until death. Thank You for my gifts and calling. Help me to develop to my full potential. Send spiritual midwives and mentors, men and women, that can pour into my life. Show me who my spiritual fathers and spiritual mothers are so that I can begin to grow in wisdom and understanding. Release to me daily discernment and the gift of discerning of spirits. Don't let me be deceived. Open my spiritual eyes and give me an understanding heart. Give me the spirit of wisdom, knowledge, understanding, counsel and might and the fear of the Lord. Let the sevenfold Spirits of God rest upon my life. Bless me, O Lord, and enlarge my territory. Bless my household (husband and children too), that we may bring You glory and honor. Bless our church and ministries where You have sent, set us and given us oversight. Let Your Kingdom come, and let Your will be done in my life. Thank You Lord for saving me and then calling me to work Your works. In Jesus Name, Amen.

Scripture References in the Prayer

Psalms 51, Psalms 139, Psalms 112, Psalms 61, Psalms 91, Acts 23:20, Romans 8:38-39, Luke 4:18-19, II Corinthians 4:9, Ephesians 5, Ephesians 4:8-16, Isaiah 11:2, Proverbs 3:3-5, Psalms 149, Matthew 25:35-36, II Corinthians 2;9, I Peter 2:9, I Corinthians 13, Joel 2:25, Deuteronomy 28:1-14, I Chronicles 4:9-10, Deuteronomy 18:9-14, Hebrews 4:12, II Corinthians 12;8, I Corinthians 4:15, Ephesians 6:10-18, II Corinthians 10:3-5,Revelation 12:10, Psalms 150, Psalms 103, Isaiah 40:31, Judges 4 and 5, Malachi 3:8-11, and Isaiah 54:17.

Chapter 23

Can We Talk?

Questions and Answers on Real Life Issues for the Hurt Lady

1. **How involved should I become in the church as a First Lady? After all, I am not the senior pastor.**

   Answer: This is something you and your husband must discuss and decide the scope of your role. If the church is small and you are trying to grow the congregation, you may need to help him a little more until God sends laborers and until you can raise up new leadership. Also you need to consider your spiritual gifts and what you can bring to enhance the ministry. Lastly, you need to make sure your home and children do not suffer from your church involvement. Your involvement will have to be balanced so the home is not neglected. Your involvement is determined by your priorities: *(God, husband, children, home, your personal needs and then the church). (Proverbs 3:5-7)*

2. **How should I respond to church conflicts when my husband is the object of discussion and attack?**

Answer: There will be church conflicts until Christ returns. Your response is always one of wisdom and discernment. You have to guard your words. Church members will use your words against you and your husband if they are unwise and spoken in anger. Your husband, the senior pastor, is the one to handle church conflicts head on. He will usually let you know how you can best support him. Your presence and prayers will have a great impact on him and the church. Always stand with him publicly. If he is wrong, handle your opinions in private. You always need a united front. I remember a church business meeting in which the pastor's wife went up and stood next to her husband. She never said a word, but they knew where she stood. I shall never forget that image in my mind of unity and oneness. The Lord will also fight your battles as long as you both are walking in obedience and righteousness to the will of the Lord. (I Samuel 17:47)

3. **There is such a temptation to compare our ministry and marriage to other ministries. Everybody else's green grass looks so much better than what God has called us to. Can you help me?**

Answer: What looks like prosperity or green grass may actually be "lean and mean." Be thankful for where God has assigned you and "work the works" and "work the Word." What He's done for others, He can do for your ministry if that is His perfect will. Read Psalms 73. The Psalmist almost "slipped" looking at the prosperity of the others. But when he finally went into the sanctuary, and got his eyes back on God, he was no longer discontent. You'll find that what God has called you to is quite fertile if you work it. Don't be tempted to become a complaining and discontented pastor's wife. You will have enough warfare to confront without adding discontent to your plate. Believe me, if another ministry or church's ministry looks greener, it's because they have paid the price in prayer and warfare, or the enemy is using magnification on you. It's okay to learn from other ministries and even from other pastoral marriages. But we must walk in the "unique assignment" God has for us. There are no shortcuts to success.

4. **Where does a pastor's wife and minister's wife find friends? It can be a lonely life since it is not wise to be chummy and common with the congregation.**

Answer: Pastor's wives, minister's wives and women in ministry have to choose their friends carefully. They must spiritually discern who to confide in because it could affect the church and the credibility of your husband's ministry. Pastor's wives must learn how to "try the spirits" of people. Also ask the Lord to connect you with other pastor's wives that over time will prove to be trustworthy. It's also good to have women outside your church as confidants. It's also wise to have a circle of intercessors praying for you and your husband that are not necessarily in the local church. God will show you whom to trust and confide in. It's important to "try the spirits by the Spirit." Many have been hurt because they could not discern the true motives of people. Even other pastor's wives proved to be untrustworthy. So, be led by the Spirit of God in all things.(I John 4: 1-4; and Isaiah 11:2)

5. **What advice would you give to a woman about to marry a minister or a pastor?**

Answer: I firstly recommend that women order my CD message called "My Prince Charming is Abusing Me." This message alerts women what to look for in men that are "so nice" but turn out to be a Dr. Jekyll, Mr. Hyde. Just being a preacher is not enough credentials to marry a man. I am finding more and more in pastoral counseling that being a "preacher" is not enough to just marry a man. Many preachers are abusers and are predators in the church. Make sure you pray and seek the Lord before marrying a minister or pastor. Meet his family. Talk to people that have known him. See how he acts under pressure and when he's angry. Do a background check. Try and spend a year or two dating him before you say you will marry him. By then, you will see all sides of him. Definitely, do not sleep with him and develop a sexual soul tie. Fornication blurs your discernment. Finally, you need to determine if your calling and ministry is compatible with his. Is this a mutual union, or are you going to have to give up much more than he does? God will confirm every concern you have. Don't compromise to get married. Don't rush into it. **If he's pressuring you, run! Ministry is tough enough without marrying a preacher that is an abuser, flaky and a fraud. Seek the Lord. (Proverbs 3)**

6. **What happens to pastor's wives that are now widowed? I don't fit in anymore since my husband is gone. What happens to my ministry?**

   Answer: First of all, you don't lose your ministry. It can now come to the forefront and as a widow you can spend more time ministering unto the Lord. Your widowhood is not the end, but it is a new beginning. If the church no longer wants you around, seek the Lord where He wants you to go and start anew and afresh. If you sense you are to remain at that church and have much to offer, then the Lord will confirm it. Your husband's book or life is closed but you are still writing new chapters in your book. It sounds like you also need to give yourself time to grieve and heal of some things. You need to realize you are not a "misfit" but you are just in a new season in your life. Also, if your identity was always tied up in your husband's identity, you will have to be healed in that area so that you can emotionally and spiritually move forward. (I Corinthians 7; Ecclesiastes 3:1-11; Isaiah 43:18-19)

7. **I am a divorced pastor's wife. How do you recommend divorced pastor's wives, minister's wives and women in**

ministry rebuild their lives and ministries?

Answer: First let me say, you may be a divorcee, but God will never divorce you. God does hate divorce but He doesn't hate you. Though your marital status has changed, your gifts and calling will still make room for you in the Body of Christ. Remember God wants to restore you. Don't get caught up in titles. Remember the "First Lady" is a title, and titles don't make you. You fit into God's plan regardless of former titles and positions. Rebuild your life again by letting God be your husband, lover and friend. Seek the Lord about the season and time of your healing. Don't try and force your way in this season. Wait upon the Lord and He will strengthen thee. Be open to change. Allow yourself time to heal, but do get deliverance and deal with your hurts and rejection. Find out who you are. You have been identified as "his wife" for so long, but now God has to restore some areas of your identity. The church can be cruel to divorcees and their families. So guard your heart during this season. Don't be afraid to be alone in this season and don't view singleness as a curse, but it is a privilege in Christ.

(Joel 2:25-26 and Isaiah 43:l8-20, Philippians 3:12-14)

8. **How should I handle women in the church that are flaunting themselves at my husband and trying to seduce him?   Should I confront these Jezebels?**

Answer: Every pastor's wife and minister's wife is confronted with a Jezebel sooner or later. As I have talked with my husband, he recommends not confronting the other woman, but letting your husband confront and put her in her place. Remember your position and that you are not only the "First Lady" but the "Only Lady." Remember that you might have to minister to that same woman, to counsel her or pray for her. Keep your spiritual eyes open and stay in your position of authority. You cannot handle a Jezebel with carnal weapons.   She must be dealt with in the Spirit realm. Pray for your husband's discernment in dealing with Jezebel, Delilah and Bathsheba type women in the church. If your husband does not want to confront her and does not handle the situation well, the problem is not the other woman, but him. Deal with your husband, not her. Also it important that you are meeting your husband's emotional and sexual needs so when these women flaunt and try to seduce, he is not tempted. Let her flaunt, but you cover your bases and take care of his needs, mental, physical and spiritual and close every gate to seduction. (Galatians 5:25 and Proverbs 5:18-21)

9. **My husband has been accused of sexual misconduct. How should I respond and what should I do? We have children and we are a high profile couple in the local community and on a national level. He has confessed to me that he's been on the "down low" with other men. I am totally humiliated.**

Answer: First of all we need to define the term *"men on the "Down low," for those who may not be familiar with the term.*

"The term is often used to describe the behavior of men who have sex with other men but do not identify openly as being gay or bisexual. These men may refer to themselves as "being on the down low"; "on the DL"; or "on the low low". The term has most often been associated with African American men. Although the term originated in the African American community, the behaviors associated with the term are not new and not specific to black men who have sex with men."

44

There seems to be a continual stream of pastors and church leaders (male and female) on a local and national level being exposed in this hour. For sure, God came to them in private first and spoke to them about their closet sins before it became public. However, God is allowing this exposure to come for your protection and the protection of the flock. There are several issues that you have to be concerned with. (1) Sexually transmitted disease. You need to get tested for STD'S and HIV infection. (2) You need to allow the church to bring him to a place of accountability (3) This is a trauma for you and the children. Separation might be an option until you can work through your marital issues. (4) If he is willing to step down and go to counseling and get help, you will have to decide if you are willing to walk with him through this difficult time.   I have seen many marriages healed when both partners are "willing" to work it out. Though you have grounds for divorce, it takes "agape love," and unconditional love, to choose to forgive and cover his faults. God will allow you to work it through and give you grace whether you stay in the marriage or not.   (5) Counseling and therapy may be needed for your children. This is going to affect them but they will take their cues based on your responses to your husband. Remember, he is still their father. (6) In this time of total humiliation, God will get you to a safe and quiet place in Him. Give yourself time to heal and seek the Lord. Get wise counsel and know "this too shall pass." My heart goes out to you and all those women of God, pastor's wives and minister's wives who have suffered in this way. Jesus our Lord identifies with you because Himself He knew what total humiliation felt like. He knew what it felt like to go through a humiliating ordeal that you did not deserve.

(Proverbs 20:22-25; Isaiah 61:8; Psalms 51)

10. **I married my husband and then he accepted his call to ministry and the pastorate. I never wanted to marry a preacher and I sure didn't want to be a "First Lady." What are my options?**

Answer: There are many women in your same situation and they feel trapped. They have found themselves fighting against God. We forget when we marry someone that many times they are still growing and evolving. We should not try to control the call of God on a person's life. Your options are few. (1) You can surrender or yield to the Hand of God on your husband's life and ask the Lord to equip you for the adventure. (2) You can resist the calling of God on his life and refuse to support him and refuse to be a spiritual partner in the next season of his life. This will bring division between you and him, and you will create another problem: God's possible judgment coming upon you. (3)You can choose not to be married to him anymore and this has happened in some cases. It's always better to not fight against what God is doing in our spouses. (4) More than likely, the fact that God has called him means that you are called also; not to his same calling or position, but to your unique calling and position. God is sovereign and He has an impeccable plan. You need to ask God what He wants you to do and what is your calling.(5) Stay away from ultimatums. Do not back yourself into a corner or make your husband feel he has to choose between you and God. You may get your feelings hurt. Ultimatums do not leave much room for ongoing discussion and working through our problems. (6) Your arms too short to box with God. Celebrate what God is doing in your husband or be found fighting against God. Real love is "unconditional" and not just on your terms. (7) Go on a fast and seek the Lord for understanding and direction. God will meet you at the place of desperation and humility. (Isaiah 6:1-9, Jeremiah 1:1-10, Isaiah 61)

11. **I did not know how much warfare I would face acknowledging my calling and ministry. I have become very bitter regarding "church folk" and how they have treated me as a woman preacher. I have been wounded by women in the church also who have persecuted and prosecuted me. How can I get healing from my hurts and bitterness and still**

serve them?

Answer: No one told us that we would get so many "hater
receptions" from church folk that are resistant to women in
ministry. We get this resistance for several reasons, but it
still hurts. It is important that you do not war against "flesh
and blood" or the saints, but you recognize you are in a fight
against demonic spirits and false teaching and ignorance. You
fight these spirits through prayer, through spreading truth and
by walking out your calling. You must get past the rejection
and resistance and know that you have not joined the "hall of
fame" but you have begun to partake of the "hall of suffering"
for the sake of Christ. Forgive them, for they know not what
they do. Begin to ask the Lord to lead you to churches and
ministries where you can get your healing and receive the
love you need to get healed. Release the bitterness, hurt, rage
and rejection. These emotions have been sent to cripple you
and your ministry. There is a grace you must learn to walk
in as you deal with persecution and prosecution. You are not
the first woman to encounter this. As you read and study
what women preachers have experienced throughout history,
you will find that you are no different. Learn from their
experiences and come out "better" and not "bitter." (Isaiah

53 and Galatians 3:28, Ephesians 4:8-16 and Ephesians 4:31)

12. **My husband and I serve as Co-Pastors. I feel that I have been given that title, but it carries no weight. I am just a co-pastor in name only with very little or no authority and power. Is being a co-pastor really biblical? The truth is, I am a prophet and my husband is an apostle. Why don't we just be biblical and call it like it is? I know I am not reaching my full potential and the church bylaws don't even address the Co-Pastor status. What should I do?**

Answer: The term "co-pastor" really is not biblical but began as a trend in the church. It is a term that began to surface in the 80's and it became a term of endearment by male pastors that recognized they were partners in ministry with their wives and they wanted to affirm the "teamwork" with their wives. This title began to allow pastor's wives a greater level of respect and bridge the gap between males and females in ministry. It represented a promotion for pastor's wives beyond sitting on the second row and wearing a hat. The title of co- pastor elevated her, for she surely was functioning in that capacity without a title. The problem lies in the fact that the church constitution did not reflect what level of power and authority she was given. Still the senior pastor had full authority and the co-pastor could serve but had to walk lightly in wielding her authority around. She had no constitutional authority. So the term co-pastor for many was a "pacification" term but carried no real authority. She was limited to certain areas of the ministry and was especially assigned to women's ministry, prayer ministry and church special projects. But many churches still are not ready for her to walk in the biblical office for which she was called, especially in traditional mainline churches. Lastly, a co-pastor term was used when a senior pastor was about to retire and he was grooming another male minister to take his place. This co-pastoring relationship was temporary, but there was really only one "main" pastor or head. It is clear that in the New Testament Church there was a "team ministry" model and there were pastors and teachers at Antioch. (Acts 13:1-3) Instead of being a co-pastor it is biblical that she serve as one of the pastors on staff among the prophets, teachers and other ministers.

The Co-Pastor Trend

The Co-pastor position is specifically designed as a short term office so that the retiring pastor and the co-pastor serve together for a short transitional period, two to three months. At the end of that period the long-time pastor retires and the "co-pastor" is installed as the pastor. They are called and installed with equal responsibility. Their pastoral duties are set by the church leadership and should they no longer serve in that position, the senior pastor continues to serve as head pastor. Most pastor's wives were never called or installed with equal responsibility and therefore it is only a term of endearment. Most of them are not paid or compensated to function as a co-pastor. So every church or denomination really defines the parameters of a co-pastor relationship of a pastor and wife. **Most churches are not ready to give equal power, equal authority and equal pay to both of you, which is really true co-pastoring.** Sometimes we jump into a trend but we do not really know what we have bought into. Trends pass with time, but what God has established in His Word will last forever. If we would just flow in our five fold offices and spiritual gifts, we would not have to get caught up in trends and fads. Eventually, we will have to get back to the Bible and the government of God. (Ephesians 4 and Acts 13:1-3)

13. **As a woman in ministry and a pastor's wife, I am committed to my husband and the ministry. I am a victim of domestic violence mostly from verbal, emotional, and financial abuse. No one knows but my children, how he**

treats me at home. A couple of times he has hit me behind closed doors. I love him but I know he needs help. He has a good heart but he is an abuser. I don't want to leave him because he is a good father and for the most part a good husband and a dynamite pastor/teacher. I realize now that I am an abused woman. How can I fix this without my husband being exposed and possibly loosing his ministry?

Answer: You are not alone. There are many women in ministry and pastor's wives and minister's wives that are battered wives. They feel trapped because of their total loyalty to God, the man, and the ministry. What would Jesus have you do? (1) **First, you have to walk in truth and admit it. You can no longer partner with the LIE.** The lie is that "this is the way marriage is and he will one day change. God wants me to be strong and bear it." That is the lie. You do have to get help for yourself. Tell someone that is totally trustworthy what you are going through. Get some deliverance and help for yourself. (2) Any church leader that is an abuser needs to step down from leadership. This would definitely send a message to the Body of Christ and to other male Christian abusers. (3) Marriage counseling is not what you need now. Your husband needs to be in counseling as an abuser and needs help for his domestic violence. It is a sin. It is a crime. It is a learned behavior. You have to address this ungodly behavior with him and let him know he has to be accountable and take responsibility for it. (4) If you decide to not "rock the boat" and keep it a secret, your children will probably become victims and become abusers themselves. Remember it is a learned behavior. One in three children that comes up in abusive homes becomes an abuser. You have to think about how this type of environment is affecting your children. (5) Be prepared to get to a safe place. You cannot fix it. Only God can fix it. I believe God will give you directions as to the steps you must take to protect yourself and the children. Keep an emergency bag ready in case you have to flee in the night. Keep some emergency money as well. Things may escalate and you will need to find quick refuge. **Remember the scripture in Ephesians 5 applies to submission only if the husband is loving you as Christ loved the Church. Never submit to violence and abuse.**

(Ephesians 5:21-33 and Psalms 91)

14. **I am a minister and wife of a pastor and I am not growing spiritually. The church is resistant to the gifts of the Spirit and of course to the five fold ministry. I believe**

that I am a prophet but I cannot be developed in my own church. Though I love the people and my Pastor, I feel like I am dying and drying up. What should I do? I don't want to be rebellious and ungrateful for my church. My heart is breaking and I am hungry for something that I cannot get here. I support my husband but he is just not able to meet my needs for spiritual growth. What can I do?

Answer: The question you must ask yourself is "do you have a false allegiance to your pastor and church?" If you know the Spirit is leading you in another direction and that you are spiritually dying where you are, you are not being rebellious in seeking to find ways to grow, You may not even need to move your membership. Begin go seek out windows of opportunity and times that you can go and be fed at seminars, conferences and even seminary training, and begin reading and studying books on your own. There is a way to grow spiritually without being rebellious where you are. Sometimes we have to go to other Houses to get what we need. It's not about being loyal to man or a denomination, it's about being obedient to God and following Him. You have already identified where you are and where they are not.

Begin to pray about where God would "replant you in this next season." It doesn't mean you are not grateful for your pastor and church family. It means that they have taken you as far as they can spiritually. We have to follow the Holy Spirit. Hopefully, you can find a "watering hole" with the blessing of the pastor/your husband for seasons of growth, without being excommunicated or looking like a traitor. I am speaking from experience, but I would rather obey God than man, and stay too long where I shouldn't be. When we stay too long three things happen. We get into disobedience; we get defiled; and we die spiritually. The choice is yours. The time is now. (Matthew 6:33 and Ephesians 4:8-16)

15. **I am a PK (preacher's kid) and I know I am called as a woman minister. I don't want to be like my parents and so I have resisted the calling. I am stuck. What should I do?**

Answer: I truly understand how you feel. Your feelings are valid, but your feelings will get you in trouble with God. Since you know you are called, you need to obey and move forward. Sounds like you have some deliverance issues from childhood with your parents, the church and your experiences as a PK. For sure God has not called you to be a carbon copy of your parents, but you should be "better and more powerful" in your generation. Don't let the enemy blind you to your rich spiritual heritage that your parents have passed on to you. Obedience is always better.

(I Peter 2:9 and John 15:16)

16. **Members are tearing down and criticizing my husband over trivial things. He is setting a new standard and he is shaking old foundations to set new order. How can I help him?**

Answer: This is always one of the most difficult things to watch your husband go through. Of course our way of helping is "on our knees in our prayer closets." Remember we are not wrestling against flesh and blood but demonic structures, demonic powers and demonic spirits. The sooner we learn to take our positions in prayer, the sooner we will see change and victory. This type of criticizing comes with the territory of pastoring. You can't please everybody and we are not supposed to try. As long as your husband is obeying the Lord, he will have that satisfaction and peace in the midst of the complainers. God will vindicate him and God will handle the murmurers. Don't pick it up and take offense. Any time

you bring change and shake old foundations there will be
retaliation. The hardest thing for pastor's wives is to remain
silent. Learn the power of "holding your tongue" and the
power of "silence." You don't need to let the congregation
know your every thought. Be a woman of few words, for this
is a sign of wisdom and self control. Choose your battles
wisely. (Philippians 2:14, Galatians 5:22-23; Isaiah 11:2)

**17. My heart is breaking over my children who have been
wounded by the things they've seen in the church. They
have begun to rebel and run away from the Lord. What
can I do after all the praying and trying to protect them all
these years?**

Answer: Our hearts do break when we see our children go
astray and become hurt by the things they have seen in the
church. No matter how much we pray, our children still have
to grow up and they have to make decisions for themselves.
If they stray, they will learn there are consequences, but our
prayers can still be a covering for them. We can continue
to pray but we have to know we have "planted the seeds of
righteousness in them " and when they grow old they will not
depart from it. Also we have to allow their relationship with

the Lord to evolve. **You can't fix it**. Just pray and allow them to mature. Some things take time to come into maturity. Continue to walk in truth and allow God to bring the increase. Hopefully your children will submit to wise counsel and ongoing deliverance. Prodigals need time, prayer, and patience in order to come back home. (Proverbs 22:6)

18. **My husband and I are in a strong traditional church but we are not traditional pastors. We are visionaries and ready for true change and for raising up a New Testament Church and not a denominational church. Is this a battle we are to fight? How do you know it's time to leave or time to stay and fight?**

Answer: My hope is that you and your husband are strong in the Lord and in the power of His might. Old traditional and religious churches are hard to pastor and hard to change. They have to be changed gradually and prayerfully. It's God's battle, not yours. Follow the blueprint of the Lord that He has given to your husband. If they won't change for God and His Word, they surely won't change for you. Sometimes an old regime has to die out, and it could be some time before you see change. You have to ask yourself the questions: (l)

Did God send us there? (2) Has His grace lifted from us
to remain here? (3) Is this a training ground for a future
assignment? (4) What is God trying to teach us as leaders and
shepherds? (5) Have we sought wise counsel on the issues we
face by those more experienced than us? (6) Are we wounded
and hurt and our vision and hearts blurred or defiled now?
(7) Have we prayed and fasted for direction from the Lord as
to whether we are to leave or stay and fight? (I Samuel 17:47)

**19. My husband is Senior Pastor and I am on staff as one of
the ministers also. He has been very supportive of me,
but I feel much of my ministry is going to take me out
of the Church into the community and involve more and
more travel. Our children are grown but I don't think the
church or our circle of friends will understand it. I don't
want it to look like I am out of order or being rebellious.
Can you speak on that?**

Answer: God is doing some very unique things this hour in
the Body of Christ and He is using clergy couples like never
before. Team ministry does not mean you are in the same
building and doing the same thing. It means you are being
used by God together for the Kingdom's sake wherever you

are assigned. You are on the same team, but not necessarily doing the same thing. Only a man that is insecure wants his wife right under him all the time. Remember, we are married, but we belong to God first. God is the Boss and decides how are gifts are best used. What looks out of order to some is not out of order for God. God's ways are not our ways. It is important that the couple know what the Lord is saying and follow the Spirit. People will always talk and gossip. But you must obey the Lord no matter how strange it looks. Coming into agreement with your spouse is key. Besides, being on the "cutting edge" means just that. God is calling for us to have "cutting edge" obedience and faith. (Psalms 128:2, Isaiah 40:31)

20. My husband is a young pastor and the church is just starting out. Though it would be great if the church could afford a full time salary for him, is it wrong for my husband to have an outside job? Is it a sin for a minister or pastor to work a secular job to support his family? How do I address him when he feels I should be happy with what the church can provide and not make him work another job?

Answer: This is a very real scenario and many pastoral marriages have ended in divorce because of this very issue. There is an old mindset or "erroneous mindset" that it is honorable for a pastor to take a vow of poverty and to suffer at the hand of a church. Some male pastors feel that since this is all the church can provide, this is God's will. Unfortunately, many churches are in the "stone age" and they do not provide ample salaries and benefits for their senior pastors. The ones who are hurt the most are the pastoral family. **It is a sin to neglect your family for the church.** If a pastor accepts a calling to a young, struggling church, he must be willing to work another job to take care of his family if the church cannot provide adequately. Sacrifice will always be needed in ministry, but God does expect our basic needs to be met. These decisions should have been worked out before you launched the church and accepted the pastorate. The family comes before the church. This is wisdom and this is biblical order. **God first, then wife and family, and then the church. (Ephesians 5)**

21. **I hear people say all the time that the "pastor has two wives, his wife and the Church". Is this biblical? I prefer to not compete with the church. Isn't this spiritual adultery?**

Answer: My husband and I discussed this "cliché" and there is nowhere in the Word of God that it implies that the pastor is married to his wife and the Church. This of course would be "bigomy" and the Bible is clear that the husband is to love his wife as Christ loved the Church. This idea came into being because the Pastor finds himself trying to please his wife and the Church (who metaphorically is a "she"). Both demand his time, both demand his attention, both need his protection and both compete for "intimacy." Many pastoral marriages have been destroyed by following this concept of two wives. It is not a biblical concept and it can become a form of spiritual adultery and begin to replace the time the pastor needs to spend with his wife and family. **Balance and priority are the keys**. The Pastor must find a balance between the two. Even a secular job or old buddies could be a form of adultery. I believe this is erroneous teaching and needs to be corrected for future generations as well. We need pastors and wives that can model what a healthy relationship between church and the First Family looks like. (Ephesians 5)

22. I consider myself somewhat of a "displaced First Lady." My husband and I divorced, but I still desire to be a

member of the church where I once was the First Lady. My husband has remarried and there is a new First Lady. Should I leave or should I stay? My children grew up there and we been part of that church family for over 20 years and poured my blood, sweat and tears into that ministry also. What should I do?

Answer: First of all, you are to be commended for even wanting to remain since you are the former First Lady. It sounds like you are not bitter and that you still have a good relationship with your husband and father of your children. I would caution you on several levels however: (1) Seek the Lord whether or not you are to remain. Just because you labored hard and long does not mean you are to stay. Remember to everything there is a season. (2) Make sure you are not hindering the new First Lady. There are people that are still loyal to you and your presence could cause division and conflict. (3) Since your ex-husband is your pastor, I am sure you can ask him how he feels about you remaining there. Ask yourself what is "best for the church?" (4) Some former First Lady's stay because their identity is tied to their ex-husband and the church. Make sure your identity is in Christ. (5) Definitely you need to move on if you have aught with your ex-husband and his new wife. Pray and ask the Lord where you need to be re-planted. Lastly, you are not displaced and the enemy wants you to feel displaced. YOU ARE JUST IN A NEW SEASON AND IT'S A GOOD SEASON. SEEK THE LORD FOR DIRECTION AND IF IT'S TIME TO MOVE ON, DON'T OVERSTAY. IF YOU BEGIN TO FEEL A RELEASE TO MOVE ON, GOD HAS GOT SOMETHING NEW AND WONDERFUL FOR YOU. **YOU PLANTED, NOW IT COULD BE TIME TO LET THE CURRENT FIRST LADY WATER IT.**

(I Cor. 3:6 and Eccl. 3:1-11)

23. **I am a female senior pastor and my husband is a deacon of the church. I am submitted to him as my husband, but he submits to me as the senior pastor. It works well for us, but some people struggle with it. The levels of spiritual warfare that I have encountered are many. How can we help other churches and some of our old associations understand? When I became the senior pastor, I lost a lot of friends and associations. I know I am in biblical order, but there are so many churches that still teach that women are to remain silent, that women are not to be in authority and that women cannot pastor. I would like to hear your**

comments on this.

Answer. (l) I could write on book on this question alone. But I will begin with Ephesians 4:8 as the best text to deal with these various views. It states that when Jesus ascended back to heaven, "he led captivity captive and He gave gifts to men." That Greek word for "men" is "anthropos" meaning humanity. This verse lets women in. Women are human beings and Christ included us in the ascension gifts which are mentioned in Ephesians 4:ll: "Now these are the gifts Christ gave to the church: the apostles, the prophets, the evangelists, and the pastors and teachers." Here we see that human beings (anthropos) can fulfill these offices. Spiritual authority is not based on gender, but it is based on whom God chooses, based on righteousness, and on being rightly equipped to fulfill it. According to Ephesians 4:8, male or female, human beings can function and flow in those five fold giftings. Now think on that. Selah.

(2) Secondly, I recognize the great levels of spiritual warfare on relationships that come against women in ministry. But it is important that you understand that as you are promoted, a separation takes place each time. Those old associations that

separated from you could not go with you to the next level. It is really their loss. Relationships will be affected for women that step into high profile leadership positions.

(3) Unfortunately there have been many texts in the Bible that are taken out of context and abused, and are used to keep women in bondage. I Corinthians 14;34-35 has been taught in error for centuries and is one of the main ways the enemy has brought spiritual warfare against women in ministry. We have to reteach and bring reformation to erroneous teaching. We have to prepare the way for other women and our daughters that are coming forth in future generations. The Apostle Paul speaks of women remaining silent in the church but it refers to "wives" or the Greek word "Gune" which means wives be silent. Wives were to ask their husbands at home certain questions regarding the scriptures because women were not taught in the early church culture, only men. It was a cultural issue as well. This text has always been taken out of context to control women. But let's just say Paul really meant this, he would not have said it was okay for women to prophesy in I Corinthians ll:5, where she is permitted to pray and prophesy. We must keep scripture in proper context. When I think about it, there is such a double standard in the Body of Christ. Many in the church don't mind women speaking up for the pastor's aide, teaching Sunday School, speaking up to raise money, but they can't

lead in real positions of authority. This is a double standard and it is not of the Lord. The other thing that grieves about this "gender war" is that there are many women in the Body of Christ who have these same views and they persecute women in leadership positions. We must pray for women in the Body of Christ to get a revelation of who they really are in Christ Jesus. **For women to persecute and "hate" on other women is to hate their own selves!**

(4) Finally, it is appropriate for a woman to be submitted to her own husband and yet when she is in a leadership position in the church, he is able to submit to her office. If a woman was elected president of the United States, she is still the wife of her husband and submitted to her own husband. But when it comes to the Office of President, she is functioning in an office and he must respect the Office of the President. We see this same principle in Judges 4 and 5 with Deborah who is a faithful wife submitted to Lapidoth her husband, but she is Judge over a nation. It is biblical and it works. Deborah was not out of order and neither are you. So be encouraged and walk in the order of God for your life. Thank God for your husband if you have a Lapidoth. It takes a powerful and secure man to not clip his "wife's wings, but allow his wife to be who God has called her to be and not be intimidated. **I have spent thirty five years of my life with such a man, Pastor Anthony W. Green.**

Chapter 24

The Legacy Award

"For our light affliction, which is but for a moment, worketh for us a far more exceeding and eternal weight of glory: while we look not at the things which are seen, but at the things which are not seen: for the things which are seen are temporal; but the things which are not seen are eternal." II Corinthians 4:17, 18. (KJV)

I love watching the Academy Awards, the Oscar Awards and the Tony Awards. I get a wonderful feeling seeing people rewarded for their hard work, their expertise, their teamwork and the fulfillment that comes with great accomplishment. As I reflected on the **Hurt Lady**, I heard the Spirit of the Lord say, **The Legacy Award**. After all the years of experience that has gone into the writing of this work, I believe the greatest reward that any of us can receive is to hear the Lord say, "Well done, my good and faithful servant," when we stand before Him. But there is something else that I don't want us to miss in all this struggle. There is yet a great work to be done in the earth before Jesus comes, and before we all get our just rewards. Even after your generation has passed on, there must be a generation that will occupy until He comes. This spiritual warfare manual is not just about the Hurt Lady, but it is a manual to insure that future generations will be able to occupy until He comes. If we are not careful, Satan being the thief that he is, will steal our **Legacy Award**.

There must be a grand finale to all that has been written and said regarding **The Hurt Lady**. As I prayed about how to close this book, I kept seeing our recent Green family photo. Our children are all grown up and even my grandchildren are in this photo. I included that photo in this chapter because I realized that everything we went through in the ministry, and everything we suffered and sacrificed for the sake of the Kingdom will not be in vain. *It is a victory photo.* We are the survivors and so are our children. Our children are the future of the Kingdom. The wounds, the warfare, and the struggles were real, but just a smokescreen. The truth is, the enemy was really after our seed all along. Satan never wanted us to survive and he wanted our children to hate the ministry and the church. He wanted to "*turn off another generation*" from serving God. Thank God I did not let my "hurt" get the best of me. **Unresolved hurt destroys us and our legacy.**

Legacy means "that which is a remaining portion, survivors, and inheritance." Every *Hurt Lady* reading this book has a legacy that she must never loose sight of. When all is said and done, we must make sure that we will have "double for our trouble." Everything that we have endured, if we come out of those years better and not bitter, God will reward us through our legacy, our children, our spiritual sons and daughters, and yes we will leave behind us a "living testimony."

There were times we got so busy doing "church work" that we almost forgot the real work was preparing and investing in our seed and future generations. Spiritual warfare always tries to distract us from the major things and drain us with the minor things. Our children are the fruit of our labor and they will carry on our legacy; for they lived with us, and they saw what was important in this life. In spite of all we went through, we passed on a rich legacy to our children of: family time, family days, the family altar, integrity, love, sacrifice, giving, suffering, sharing, work, struggle, music and instruments, Sunday dinners, birthdays, chores and responsibility, education and achievements, rewards for good grades, miracles, worship and prayer, laughter, holidays, hospitality, and how to walk in real spiritual authority. They saw our marriage and ministry weather the good times and the hard times. And when all was said and done, ***there was still enough love to go around.***

At the end of the day, the real test of our effectiveness in marriage, parenthood and ministry is not a big building left behind with our name on it. It will be the legacy we leave behind in the lives that we have touched and those lives that were transformed into the image of Christ.

Satan wanted our focus to be on "all the hell we went through" and not the fact that we were raising up warriors and faithful priests that would not give up or give in when the gates of hell tried to prevail in their generation.

We cannot stay hurt or wounded for too long, or we will be consumed and forget about our legacy. So we must arise and keep raising up strong righteous seeds and true spiritual sons and daughters to carry the legacy of truth of the of Gospel of Jesus Christ. "Church members don't carry on the legacy, but spiritual sons and daughters do." We must keep investing in those that will carry the Gospel to the ends of the earth and fulfill the Great Commission.

When I looked at our family picture, I saw the Legacy Award. For in the face of my children and grandchildren, I can see that which my husband and I labored most for. **It was the legacy. It was our seed. It was our spiritual sons and daughters the enemy was really after. It was our love for the lost.** But it's all been worth it to be wounded and scarred so that our legacy would carry on the Kingdom work. What a blessing to live to see them arise as righteous standard bearers in their generation. What a blessing to have all our children serving either in the local church, the marketplace or going to the nations of the world.

The Church can no longer afford to lose any of our righteous seed to the world, and we cannot afford to stay wounded and hurt too long. We know now that those hurts and wounds are just "light afflictions" that last for a moment, and we must never lose sight of the far more exceeding and eternal weight of glory.

At the close of this book, you will find me "about My Father's business."

At the end of the day, I am still "my sister's keeper."

And when I stand before the Lord to receive my rewards, the Legacy Award will also include every *Hurt Lady* that became a *Healed Lady*.

The Green Family Legacy Today

(Photo used by Permission of Lasting Impressions Photography,

Redlands, CA, 2007)

Pastor Anthony and Bishop Dr. Jackie Green Celebrating 35 Years in Team Ministry and 35th Wedding Anniversary.

Photo used by Permission of Lasting Impressions Photography, Redlands, California, 2007

End Notes

Introduction

1. **J. Lee Grady,** *10 Lies the Church Tells Women: How the Bible Has Been Misused to Keep Women in Spiritual Bondage (Lake Mary, Florida: Charisma House:2000):p 10.*

Chapter 2

2. **Jackie L. Green,** *Women as Bishops, Understanding the Ministry of the Overseer (Phoenix, Arizona, JGM-National PrayerLife Institute:2006):p.l5.*

3. **Ibid.,** *p. 11.*

4. **Ibid.,** *p. 12.*

Chapter 3

5. **Chuck D. Pierce and Rebecca Wagner Sytsema,** *The Future War of the Church (Ventura, California: Renew Books: 200l):pp. 256-266.*

6. **Weptanomah W. Carter,** *The Black Minister's Wife (Baltimore, Maryland Ministry of Books:1990):p. 87.*

7. **J. Lee Grady,** *10 Lies the Church Tells Women, p.211.*

Chapter 4

8. **Jackie L. Green, CD** *Message: Balancing Marriage, Motherhood and Ministry, (Phoenix, AZ: JGM National PrayerLife Institute:2000)*

9. **Reverend Al Miles,** *Domestic Violence, What Every Pastor Needs to Know (Minneapolis, MN, Augsburg Fortress Press: 2000): p.127.*

10. **Ibid.,** *p. 126.*

Chapter 5

11. **Gayle Haggard and Becky Hunter,** *Depression Hits Some Pastor's Wives News Article (Associate Press, Selma, Tennessee: 2006)*

Chapter 6

12. **Richard A. Murphy,** *Article: Statistics About Pastors, Global Pastor's* Network, (Donna, Texas: Marantha Life: 2002).

13. **Jackie L. Green,** *Teaching on Spiritual Warfare101, (Phoenix, AZ JGM-National PrayerLife Institute: 2005).*

14. **Jackie L. Green,** *Mental Warfare, Helping Intercessors Develop a Mind for Spiritual Warfare (Phoenix, AZ- JGM-National Prayerlife Institute: 2007): pp. 14-16.*

15. **Jackie L. Green,** *Spurned Into Apostleship,* (*Bloomington, Indiana, Author House Publishers: 2006):pp. 84-85.*

Chapter 8

16. **Reverend Al Miles,** *Domestic Violence, What Every Pastor Needs to Know (Minneapolis, MN, Augsburg Fortress Press: 2000): p.59-60.*

17. **Pastor Talbert W. Swan, II.** *The Church and Domestic Violence Article,* <u>www.afampointofview.com</u>*:2007)*

18. **Ibid., Talbert W. Swan, II.,** <u>www.afampointofview.com</u>.

Chapter 9

19. **Reverend Al Miles,** *Domestic Violence, What Every Pastor Needs to Know (Minneapolis, MN, Augsburg Fortress Press: 2000): p.122.*

20. **Jackie L. Green,** *CD Message: My Prince Charming is Abusing Me (Phoenix Arizona, New Generation Christian Fellowship Church:2007)*

21. **Reverend Al Miles, p.** *75.*

22. **Ibid.,** *p. 23.*

23. **Ibid.,** *p. 44.*

24. **Ibid.,** *p. 49.*

25. **Jackie L. Green,** *CD Message: My Prince Charming is Abusing Me (Phoenix Arizona, New Generation Christian Fellowship Church:2007.***26. Ibid.,** *Jackie L. Green (CD Message)*

Chapter 10

27 **Anthony and Jackie Green,** *Deliverance for Children, Loose*

the Lambs, (Phoenix, Arizona, JGM-National PrayerLife
Institute: 2003:, p. 11.

Chapter 11

28 **Rick Godwin,** *Exposing Witchcraft in the Church, (Orlando,
Florida,* Creation House Publishers:1997): p. 5.

29. **Rick Joyner,** *Epic battles of the Last Days, (Charlotte NC,
Whitaker* Hous:,1995:.p.l03.

30. **Jim W. Goll,** *The Seer (Shippensburg, PA, Destiny Image
Publisher:,* 2004):p. 86.

Chapter 12.

31.   **J. Lee Grady,** *10 Lies the Church Tells Women, p.122.*

32.   **Jackie L. Green,** *Women as Bishops, p. 22.*

Chapter 13

33. **Vashti M. McKenzie,** *Not Without a Struggle, Leadership
Development For African American Women in Ministry
(Cleveland, OH, United Church Press: 1996: p 113.*

34.   **Chuck D. Pierce and Rebecca Wagner Sytsema,** *The Future
War of the Church, Ventura, CA, Renew Books:2001):p. 244.*

35.   **Ibid.,** *p. 265.*

36. **Vashti M. McKenzie,** *Not Without a Struggle, Leadership
Development* For African American Women in Ministry
(Cleveland, OH, United Church Press: 1996: p 10.

Chapter 14

37. **Reverend Al Miles,** *Domestic Violence, What Every Pastor Needs to Know*

(*Minneapolis, MN, Augsburg Fortress Press: 2000): p.139.*

38. **Ibid.,** *p. l42.*

39. **Jackie L. Green,** *Spurned Into Apostleship*, (*Bloomington, Indiana, Author House Publishers: 2006):pp. 127-128..*

40. **Jackie L. Green,** *Kingdom Marriages Manual, 30 Ways to Build Intimacy* By Anthony and Jackie Green, (Phoenix, Arizona, JGM-National PrayerLife Institute: 2007):p 62.

Chapter 15

41. **Jackie L. Green**, *Stolen Identity Chart, Sermon: I Am My Sister's Keeper, (Phoenix, Arizona: JGM-National PrayerLife Institute, 2008)*

Chapter l6

42. **Jackie L. Green,** *Birthing and Building Ministry in Believers (Phoenix, Arizona, JGM-National PrayerLife Institute: 1999): pp. 13-17*

Chapter 19.

43. **Vashti M. McKenzie,** *Not Without a Struggle, Leadership Development* For African American Women in Ministry (Cleveland, OH, United Church Press: 1996).

Chapter 23

44. Mark Cichocki, R.N., *What Is Meant by Men on the Down-Low? About.com, July 9, 2007.*

Scripture Index

Romans 12:2
I Corinthians 1:30
II Corinthians 10:4-5
Galatians 1:4
Ephesians 2:6
Ephesians 6:10-18
Philippians 4:6
Philippians 4:13
Colossians 1:13
I Timothy 1:7
I John 4:4
Revelation 12:11

Chapter 7
II Corinthians 4:8

Chapter 10
Genesis 18:19
Exodus 20:7
Deut. 6:7
Deut. 31:21
Deut. 32:5
I Samuel 1:27-28
I Samuel 3:19-21
Psalms 14:1
Psalms 25:21
Psalms 78:8
Proverbs 11:3
Proverbs 20:12-13
Proverbs 20:31
Proverbs 22:6
Proverbs 30:11
Isaiah 28:9-10
Isaiah 59:2
Jeremiah 1:10
Jeremiah 9:20-21
Jer. 18:21, 29:11

Hosea 4:6
Malachi 4:5-6
Matthew 6:5-33
Matthew 16   Acts 20:24
Matthew 16:9
Matthew 17:17
Luke 2:52
Romans 12:2
I Corinthians 1:30
II Corinthians 10:4-5
Galatians 1:4
Ephesians 2:6
Ephesians 6:10-18
Philippians 4:6
Philippians 4:13
Colossians 1:13
I Timothy 1:7
I John 4:4
Revelation 12:11

Chapter 7
II Corinthians 4:8

Chapter 10
Genesis 18:19
Exodus 20:7
Deut. 6:7
Deut. 31:21
Deut. 32:5
I Samuel 1:27-28
I Samuel 3:19-21
Psalms 14:1
Psalms 25:21
Psalms 78:8
Proverbs 11:3
Proverbs 20:12-13
John 3:16

Acts 8:33
1 Cor. 6:20
2 Cor. 10:4-5
2 Cor. 10:12-14
Ephesians 1:11
Ephesians 6:10-18
Philippians 3-4
Colossians 2:8
I Timothy 1:6-7
I Timothy 4:12
II Timothy 1:7
Hebrews 1:4
I Peter 2:9
I Peter 3:9
I John 5:11-12

Chapter 11
Deut. 18:9-13
I Samuel 15:23
I Kings 18:38
Psalms 27:1
Proverbs 1:7
Proverbs 30:5
Isaiah 11:2
Jeremiah 23:29-30
Matthew 16:19
Galatians 3:1
Galatians 5:19-31
Ephesians 6:10-18
Philippians 2:10-11
Hebrews 4:12
Revelation 12:11

Chapter 12
Genesis 29:9
II Chronicles 32:5
Psalms 121

Isaiah 6:1-9
Isaiah 11:2
Isaiah 40:31
Isaiah 43:18-19
Isaiah 53
Isaiah 61
Isaiah 61:8
Jeremiah 1:1-10
Joel 2:25-26
Matthew 6:33
John 15:16
Acts 13:1-3
I Corinthians 3:16
I Corinthians 7
I Corinthians 11:5
I Corinthians 14:34-35
Galatians 3:28
Galatians 5:22-23
Galatians 5:25
Ephesians 4:8-16
Ephesians 4:31
Ephesians 5
Ephesians 5:21-33
Philippians 2:14
Philippians 3:12-14
I Peter 2:9
I John 4:1-4

Chapter 24
II Corinthians 4:17-18

Appendices

APPENDIX A

Hurt Lady Personal Survey

Check off areas that reflect your present season in life.

_____1. I am experiencing resistance, rejection or rebellion by others to my role of the pastor's wife or co-pastor or woman in ministry.

_____2. I have not discovered my gifts and calling in Christ yet. I am still searching for my identity.

_____3. I am not as equipped as I should be in leadership and spiritual warfare. I need to be better trained and equipped.

_____4. I am trying to walk in the footsteps of former first ladies and being under constant comparison. I have not made my mark yet as the First Lady.

_____5. I am not properly covered and protected by my husband who is the pastor.

_____6. I am living in the parsonage, in the fish bowl, and dealing with living under

limitations of lack and lack of privacy needed to develop our home.

_____7.   I have had a hard financial season and the church/ministry

is also struggling financially but I am believing God for the

breakthrough.

_____8.   I have tried to warn my husband of the seductions in

progress but he has not heeded to my warnings.

_____9.   I am under a scope and feel stressed and feel that I have to

dress the best and be the perfect First Lady and wife.

_____10. I am wearing too many "hats" to fill in church vacancies

and needs. I am not even compensated for my expertise just

because I am the pastor's wife.

_____11.   I have had to protect my children from the wolves and

church politics. I am taking the hits for them so they won't

really see the church for what it is.

_____12.   I have no one to talk to about my marital problems or my

personal issues.

_____13.   I am neglecting my own personal and spiritual growth

and development to help my husband and the church benefit.

_____14.   I think I have developed a false obligation to the church

and it is not healthy

_____15.   I feel that I am more and more isolated and depressed

being a pastor's wife

____16.   I am struggling trying to balance marriage, motherhood and ministry.

____17 .   I feel I can't trust too many people. I need God to increase my discernment and give me the discerning of spirits.

____18.   I do not have an armor bearer or strong women of God to help me.

____19.   I am not knowledgeable about the occult and witchcraft but I think it is working in the midst of the congregation and against my family

____20.   I feel my true identity has been stolen by the title of First Lady. I don't really know who I am and my identity is tied up in my husband's.

____21.   I am concerned that there are no benefits or security for me or the children if my husband become incapacitated or dies in the pastorate.

____22.   I am a divorced, wounded and bitter former First Lady. My life has been destroyed almost by the church and my children will never be the same.

____23   I don't want to be a pastor's wife or minister's wife. I feel I married the man but I didn't marry the ministry.

____24.   I am a single woman of God in ministry. I need a spiritual mentor and I need ongoing deliverance from past hurts and failures so I can be more balanced.

_____25. I am a battered pastor's wife. I need help but I don't know which way to go.

_____26. I am a single woman in ministry, and I crossed the sexual boundaries with a lesbian woman. I am not a lesbian, but I feel trapped now. Help me please.

_____27. I am a woman in the church that was molested by a male leader in the church.

I need counseling, deliverance and direction for my life.

_____28. I am a single divorced female minister and I have raising a child. I get lonely but can't afford to get tied up with another Prince Charming.

_____29. I am a wounded female Pastor and I need personal ministry from deep hurts.

_____30. I have not found a church home that I feel my ministry can flourish in yet. I feel like a misfit at times. I need guidance and spiritual mentoring.

_____31. My husband is a pastor and we need some marriage counseling. We need to find someone we can trust and confide in.

APPENDIX B

Journaling...A Method of Healing for the Hurt Lady

Journaling is a spiritual discipline to help us hear the *Voice of God* and see the divine patterns that God designed for our lives from the foundations of the earth. Journaling also helps you work through deep hurts, and reflect on the lessons that God wants us to learn from our trials and tribulations. It is an invaluable tool to help us reflect and look at our hearts and also see the heart of God.

Journaling helps you to:

1. Pray more effectively and more focused

2. Keep a record of dreams and visions

3. Keep a record of your prophetic words

4. Keep a record of directions from the Lord

5. Build your daily discipline in hearing and seeking the Lord

6. Uncover and unveil the tricks and plots of the enemy over long periods of time

7. Get still before the Lord

8. Build your expectation for hearing the Voice of the Lord

9. Build your discernment

10. Hold on to the promises of God against all odds

11. Meditate and contemplate on the deep things of God

12. See the record of victories of trusting the Lord

13. Focus in times of fasting and prayer

14. Pay attention to details and learn the ways of the Lord

15. Visualize entrepreneurial ideas and ideas for witty inventions

16. Keep a record of sermons that you've heard and sermons that you've birthed

17. See the progress you have made through the years

18. Store and retrieve information that you need at the appointed time of unveiling

19. Show the Lord how serious you are about everything He says and reveals to you

20. Pass on precious information to the next generation

21. Reflect and heal from past hurts and wounds

22. Discover your true self and who God is calling you to be

APPENDIX C

Demonic Spirits Assigned To the Hurt Lady

Abandonment
Abortion
Abuse
Accuser of the brethren
Addiction
Adultery
Anger/Rage
Anxiety
Apathy
Argument
Assault
Batterer
Bat spirit (drainer)
Betrayal
Bewitchment
Bitterness
Bitter root
Bitter gall

Down low
Embarrassment
Empty shell
Enabler
Error
Escape
Exhaustion
Failure
False burdens
False friends
False prophecy
False teaching
False transition
Fantasy
Fear
Fixer
Flattery
Frigidity

Misogyny
Neglect
Nervous breakdown
Oppression
Opposition
Panic attacks
Past
Perversion
Pharmekia
Prostitution of gifts
Poverty
Prince Charming
Rejection
Rebellion
Religious spirits
Resentment
Recall (memory)
Secrets

© 2008, Compiled by Bishop Dr. Jackie L. Green, JGM-NPI

Blackball
Blocking spirits
Bondage
Broken dreams
Broken heart
Captivity
Castaway
Competition
Confusion
Control
Darkness
Death
Debate
Deep Hurt
Denominati onalism
Deception
Deep Hurt
Depression
Despair

Destruction
Displacement
Dissatisfaction
Division
Divorce

Gloom
Gluttony
Greed
Guilt
Harassment
Hidden hurt
Hell hounds
Identity theft
Ignorance
Infirmity
Insecurity
Isolation
Intimidation
Invisible
Jealousy
Jezebel
Lack
Lesbianism
Loneliness

Low self esteem
Lust
Mammon
Male
Migraines

Seduction
Self Hatred
Sexism
Sexual Harassment
Shame
Slander
Suicide
Threatenings
Traditions of men
Torment
Unforgiveness
Unworthiness
Vain imaginations
Vanity
Witchcraft
Worry
Wounded Spirit

*Bind marriage breaking spirits
and home wrecker spirits also.

APPENDIX D

12 Commandments to Keep Your Deliverance

(How to Keep Demons from Returning)

© Copyright, 2006, by Dr. Jackie L. Green, JGM-NPI

1. **Thou shall get** rid of anything that could give legal entry for the

    demons to return. (items, occult items, books/'videos/etc.,)

    Acts 19:17-20

2. **Thou shall put** yourself on a daily diet plan of Bible (intake)

    daily, prayer, fasting, and meditation on the Word to keep

    yourself strengthened. Set an altar in your home and anoint

    yourself and home regularly. Have someone that you are

    accountable to in helping you walk through your deliverance

    process. (*Joshua 1:8, 24:15*)

3. **Thou shall break** off unholy relationships immediately that have

    been part of your previous bondage. If you are in a home

    and have to live in the midst of old temptations, sanctify your

    own room/area and ask God for a protective shield against

those areas and to open the door for you to move out of the situation. (*II Corinthians 6:17*)

4. **Thou shall confess daily** your healing and deliverance that you have received and overcome the enemy by sharing your testimony with others whenever opportunity presents itself. (*Rev. 12:11 and Romans 8:l*)

5. **Thou shall not** live by your "feelings" but by faith and by the Word of God. (*Galatians 3:3*)

6. **Thou shall not** look back at your past but press forward to fulfill your destiny. Do not allow the Devil to bring up your past, but cast those negative thoughts and accusations down. (*Philippians 3:13, 14*)

7. **Thou shall avoid** and run for your life from your "kryptonite" like Superman did or from your the habitual sins. If you should fall back into sin, confess it immediately and receive God's forgiveness, perfect love and cleansing. *I John l:9*

8. **Thou shall be filled** with the Holy Spirit and let Him take control of every area of your life. (*Romans 12:1-2*)

9. **Thou shall not fear** but be filled with faith and courage. (*II Corinthians 7:5, Ps. 34:4*)

10. **Thou shall not get the "big head"** and think you've got it made, but be alert to the sneaky traps and entry points of the devil to trap you again. Next time you let devil the back into

those cleansed areas, he will bring seven more demons more deadly, so fight to keep them returning for they will be seven times harder to get rid of. *(Hebrews 13:5 and Luke 11:24-26)*

11. **Thou shall continue** to go through deliverance and deal with other areas in your life, and not being deceived into thinking that demons will never bother you again. We *live in a world that is not a "demon free zone"* **but we can limit their activity.** *(Eph.6:10-l7)*

12. **Thou shall be thankful** unto God and bless His Name more than you talk about Satan and his tricks. Remember greater is He that is in you than he (the Devil) that is in the world.

Rejoice always, I say rejoice.
(Psalms l03:6, Phil. 4;8 and I John 4

APPENDIX E

OCCULT and New Age TERMS

(Excerpt from <u>Deliverance Team Training Manual</u> by Dr. Jackie L. Green)

Atheist- A pagan, someone who doesn't believe in the existence of God

antichrist spirits- Any spirit that is against the Word of God or the principles of the Bible and hates Jesus Christ, denouncing His deity as the Son of God, come in the flesh.

Astral Projection- When the physical body lies dormant and the astral (spirit) body travels or supernaturally projects through a medium putting them in a trance. The occult teaching says that one's soul can leave the body, travel at will anywhere, then re-enter the body. Both soul and body are claimed to remain connected by a cord.

Astrology– A very familiar form of divination by forth telling a person's future and getting direction from the influence of stars and planets for their human affairs. (Horoscopes, Zodiac signs, Life Path Reports, Dream analysis, gemstones, to name a few)

Aura– The demonic shield or presence around persons that has opened themselves up to the occult, or the third eye. Usually persons that are involved in divination can spot persons with an aura and read the rainbow of colors that are said to radiate around the person. Christians do not and should have an "aura" about them, but they have the glory of the Holy Spirit radiating from them.

Automatic Writing- When a person puts themselves into a deep trance and allows a demonic spirit to move their arm or hands to write down information from a dead persons that they are trying to communicate with.

Bewitch- to be under the power or spell or influence of an evil spirit

Black Magic– Magic sent forth for evil purposes

Candle Magic- Magic by use of candles according to candle colors for specific outcomes and usually an incantation is done with candle burning.

Channelling- Voluntary spirit-possession where a demonic spirit enters the body and speaks as a spiritual guide to or through the person. Many occultists know that these demon spirits will trick, lie and even injure their customers. These demon spirits are invited in through involvement in drugs, meditation, yoga, transcendental meditation™ , hypnosis, ouija boards and séances.

Contagious Magic- Magic based on the relationship and contact of persons to influence them with objects (performing rites over their hair, fingernails, or personal belongings) to curse the person.

Chanting- To repeat syllables or words in a monotone to conjure up and make contact with the spirit world or idol gods

Chain Letters– A curse in action or a form of bringing good luck if you follow the instructions of the letter. This is a form of "charm" and releases a threat of calamity or destruction to the person if they don't participate or it promises good luck if you do. It is really a waste of time and should be torn up immediately. It is a scheme for many and a false web of hope.

Clairvoyance- A counterfeit word of knowledge and form of divination. It is to see an inner or mental picture given by a demonic power which usually relates to health or personal problems. This is frequently practiced by Spiritualist churches to aid in healing and is a form of witchcraft.

Cockatrice—Found in the scriptures and was used several times in the King James Bible to translate one of the Hebrew words for 'serpent'. It had a head and legs of a cock, but the body and tail of a small dragon and was venomous.

Like some people it could kill people with its deadly glance. It was said to come from an egg laid by a <u>cock</u> (or from a duck's egg) hatched out by a <u>toad</u>. It is considered a demonic spirit that we deal with in spiritual warfare, called the "evil eye" and it is compared to a person that drops eggs of discord in the Body of Christ that hatch later after the person has left the church and caused division and schism.

Coven- A close knit group working together for the purpose of practicing witchcraft or rebellious activities against the ordained order of the Word of God. They meet for the structure, training programs to become priests and priestesses in the occult. They draw power from their pagan gods, the universe or nature. Coven membership(dedication or initiation depending on the tradition) is not something to be entered into lightly. It is not a church and it is not a club. They are pagan groups held together by the master deceiver, Satan. **A coven can also be defined as an unauthorized prayer group or secret group in the church that is in rebellion to the set order of the House. They pray against the vision and purposes of God and try to overthrow set authorities in their own church. (mutiny).**

Crystals– A New Age belief that gems or stones possess mystical, esoteric, spiritual powers or energy to bring the person health, wealth and good luck.

Crystalmancy– Divination by using crystals even causing a type of hypnosis to see visions in the crystals.

Curse- The opposite of blessing. A curse means to speak evil against, to utter or call forth mischief or injury to cause that person or persons to fall; an evil desire to bring people into great calamities and destruction. To work evil deeds and encantations against someone or something, to bring about illness, destruction or death.

Diva- Goddess. Usually this a woman who refers to herself as one to be worshipped. Diva comes from the word **divination.** Many Christian women today are calling themselves divas and see themselves as goddesses in their various fields (music, modeling, Gospel Music etc)

Divination- To obtain knowledge by forbidden magical means; to see into the spirit world illegally or outside the Holy Spirit of god. Divination is seeking information from demons.

Dungeons and Dragons— An occult fantasy role playing game using demon names and witchcraft spells. It teaches basic witchcraft practices and demon possession to the players, usually kids and teens.

Fetish— The act of cursing objects by assigning evil spirits to those objects to affect persons negatively that acquire the objects. (statues, rabbit's foot, clothing, jewelry, collectables)

Fire Walking- To be in a trancelike state and to "dare to do the impossible" by walking through the fire bare footed and not being burned or feeling pain because a demon power has inhabited the person. The Bible speaks against "passing through the fire" in Deut 18.

Freemasons— Probably the most influential cult in the world, founded in 1717 in London. Men of every faith and creed are accepted as a brother in this lodge. The holy book of every religion is deemed equal to the Bible, and the gods and prophets of those religions all claim to be equal to each other, regardless to how they contradict each other. Many Christians, including pastoral leaders, are Masons and have taken secret oaths that open them up to bloodline curses and hinder the growth of the Gospel, by making them unable to receive certain revelation and moves of God's Spirit in their churches and region.

Goddess- the belief that the divine is feminine, or that there are female deities or that all women are divine, and they are goddesses.

Gothic Teens— A vampire cult; youth that become creatures of the night, with a propensity for wearing black. Some file their teeth and join vampire clubs. They bite each other's necks and arms until they draw blood and they drink it. Drinking blood is often found in black magic practices such as Satanism. (Lev. 7:26-27 forbids this) They gather in the graveyards and cemeteries at night and are fascinated with death, immortality, the mysterious, forbidden sexuality, sexual power, rebellion and violence.

The Gathering- An occult role playing card game. Cards are divided into categories such as creatures and sorcery, enchantments, spells and monsters. It teaches youth how to cast spells.

Hex- A spell to bring death, harm or misfortune.

Hypnosis- To allow yourself to fall into a deep trance or altered state of consciousness and thusly give another person control over your subconscious mind, opening yourself up to demons and occult power.

Imaginary Friend- A spirit guide that is trying to attach itself to your child. Listen to your children if they say they have an imaginary friend. Some spirit guides come now through the bloodline from generation to generation, a familiar spirit that has demonized the bloodline.

Incantation- A formula that is spoken or sung as a ritual to send curses or worship idol gods.

Incubus and Succubus- Evil spirits that lie with individuals while they are sleeping, that may try to have sexual intercourse with while they sleep, oppress and burden them, and cause nightmares. Incubus attacks females and succubus attacks males. They can cause lustful dreams.

Invocation– The calling forth of demons or to invite a god

Kachina Dolls– Katchina comes from the ancestral religion of the Hopi, Zuni and Pueblo tribes of the present day Arizona and New Mexico Native American tribes. They believe that when people die, their spirits are transformed into kachinas, that then make their home in the underworld, the place of departed souls. Kachinas or kachinam represent myths and there are more than 250 kachinas. Hopi and Zuni are known for their carved wood kachina dolls which represented departed spirits. After a ceremonial dance, the children receive these dolls and are encouraged to identify with the ancestral spirits represented by the dolls.

Karate- (Martial Arts)- Karate means "empty hand" and its primary purpose is to unite mind, body and spirit to achieve the unity envisioned by Zen Buddhism.

Kundalini– means "serpent power" that is unleashed in the lives of persons that practice Middle Eastern religions and martial arts, yoga and other occult forms.

Magic– to use or invoke demonic power to control and manipulate people, situations, weather or whatever evil purpose is trying to be accomplished by deceptive techniques, formulas, potions or ceremonies.

Magnification-to blow out of proportion or make something bigger than it really is. Demonic magnification is used by Satan and by evil workers to exaggerate and overstate an issue and to make a thing or situation look worse than it really is.

Martial Arts– the word "martial" means militant or eager to fight. It is not just a technique for fighting, but expressions of Eastern religious philosophy. Martial arts is an open door to gain great psychic powers. The spirit again of Kundalini enters in and the goal is to achieve perfect balance with the gods.

Money Magic- Sorcery by formulas and spells spoken or chanted over money to bring increase or destruction; to cast spells over money to bring a desired end by controlling the outcome. Also money magic is used to curse church finances or curse whatever comes in contact with the coins or dollar bills.

New Ager- A person that is involved in one of three levels in New Age activities; (1) Occasional Dabbler, (2) Regular Experimenter and (3) Hard Core.

New Age- (NAM) New Age Movement– an old lie in a new package and it is an antichrist set of beliefs that has filled the earth since the fall of Adam and Eve. New Age can be defined as any person, place, thing, teaching movement, religion or mindset tht is contrary to the Word of God or that has become an alternative solution to the Word of God to fulfill their spiritual needs. Satan is the founder and perpetrator of the New Ageism.

New Age Music- Music that is produced by New Agers with the intent to cause one's mind to drift and promote relaxation to meditate and even flow into hypnosis. Some New Age music is produced with ethno tribal overtones and are used to caress the mind and elevate various moods.

Necromancy– A form of divination used when a human being (as a medium) seeks to contact the spirits of the dead in order to obtain information about the future. Ouija boards and séances are the most common methods of necromancy.

Numerology- To tell one's future by the significance of numbers, or to calculate their sums, totals etc., and tell fortunes by using numbers.

Occult- The word occult comes from the Latin word *occultus* meaning clandestine, hidden or secret, referring to knowledge of things hidden and forbidden by the Word of God. Occultism is the study of occult and hidden wisdom, which can involve such subjects as magic or magick, extra-sensory perception, astrology, spiritualism, numerology and many other New Age philosophies and practices. The goal of the occult is to gain power and use demonic power over situations and people they want to control or influence.

Omen- A sign, or person, place or thing or event regarded as a sign of future good or evil.

Palm Reading- Fortune telling by reading the lines of the palms of the hands to tell your future.

Ouija Board- A board game that is an occult tool to trick and ensnare the curious into contact with demonic familiar spirits. This games opens people up to the invisible demonic forces that can lead to heavy occult bondage.

Pendulum and Divining Rods- Items used by many alternative healers. Divining rods are usually sticks or wires in the hand to locate water or precious metals by psychic powers working in that person.

Poltergeists- A German word for "noisy or rattling ghost" or a mischievous spirit or form of energy or noisy spirit. It describes a phenomena which includes banging, levitating furniture, strange sounds, movement of objects around a house, disappearance of objects which turn up again suddenly, sudden appearance of small objects, stones, coins, spontaneous appearance of writing and drawing on a wall or furniture or paper, random vandalism and destruction of household objects, rearrangement of household items into neat patterns and people feeling they have been pushed by an invisible force. Usually a ghost or evil spirit is linked to an object or person that was in the dwelling place.

Potion Magic- The use of liquids, oils and potions used to cast spells. A person may even wear certain oils or fragrances to lure the person to them, also putting certain powders in food to work magic on individuals.

Psychic- An occult or New Age medium or practitioner who gains knowledge from spirit guides or demons.

Reiki- A method of occult healing touch. It is claimed that through the laying on of hands a higher frequency of powerful cosmic healing energy can be tapped into. Practitioners are initiated by a Reiki Master and there is a transmission of occult power. This has nothing to do with the Bible and laying on of hands according to the Word

Reincarnation- A false New Age Hindu belief that when a person dies they have the ability to come again to earth, inhabit a new body, and live as many lives as they want or need.

Santeria- Santeria or La Regla Lucumi, orginated. in West Africa in what is now Nigeria and Benin. It is the traditional religion of the Yoruba people. The slave trade caused Santeria, a new age religion, to spread to Cuba, Brazil, Haiti, Trinidad, Puerto Rico and other places. They worshipped the god Olorun and Olodumare where they receive spiritual energy. Santerian religion is famous for it's magic based on the knowledge of mysteries or orishas.

Seance– Attempting to contact the dead through the use of a group gathering and the assistance of a medium They are actually contacting demonic spirits and not the dead person or relative. Biblically it is impossible to consult the dead, as they are either in heaven or hell and there is a great gulf between the dead and the living. Luke 16:22-25

Shaman– A shaman is a priest or priestess (not of the Most High God) who uses occult practices to cure the sick, divine the unknown and control events. They operate in the unseen world of the gods, demons and ancestral spirits which they summon. Shamans can manipulate the weather, drive away evil sprits and counter attack spells and demonically cure the sick and escort souls to the underworld. A shaman can be called a satanic priest or priestess, a witch or a witchdoctor, a medicine man, sorcerer, magician or guru.

Soothsayer– A person that is a medium psychic, witch, warlock, wizard or sorcerer.

Sorcery- The practice of magick or magic, usually involving drugs, potions and spells.

Soul mate- A New Age term used to define persons that yoke themselves with someone in a relationship based on occult and New Age matchmaking formulas. Christians do not have souls mates. Soul mates are bound together by evil soul ties and deceptive tactics and motives. It is not a biblical term. The Bible does speak of soul ties between David and Jonathan, but they were not soul mates. Also, as you study soul mates in the New Age community, you will find that they fall out of "soul mating" after they tire of one another and move on to find another partner.

Spell– To charm or seduce the mind of a person to the point they are fascinated, blinded or distracted from truth.

Spirit Guide– A demonic spirit assigned to guide and direct a person when they open themselves up to divination, imaginary friends and counseling from psychics. Spirit guides convince people that they have access to tremendous amounts of wisdom and knowledge for their lives. Spirit guides go by another name such as: a friend, wise one, an inner counselor, an inner healer, a master, a higher self, an angel of light, ascended master

Spiritualist– A medium or one that contacts the dead on behalf of the living.

Tarot Cards– Tarot cards are used in fortune telling and are considered divination. These cards are used by fortune tellers as well as to tell a person's future. Tarot cards are popular among occultist and New Agers in all walks of life.

Third Eye- The realm of psychic power by which a person sees illegally into the spirit world. Sometimes called the All-Seeing Eye or Eye of Horus or Eye of Ra. this eye can be seen in many pictures as an eye in the center of the forehead of an individual and some people even tattoo an eye on their forehead or back of the head. The third eye is also referred to as the sixth sense or extra sensory perception.

Vex- to irritate or to agitate in a petty or nagging way

Wicca- A New Age religion, which is a mixture of occult and witchcraft, nature worship, female goddesses, paganism and neo-paganism.

Wile- A trick of the devil

Wi tch-Usually referring to a female that is a practitioner of the divination and sorcery (a psychi, a channeler, a sorcerer., a palm reader) A witch can also be a person who has the

Spirit of a Witch- A Christian that is in rebellion and using manipulation to further their agenda in the church or wherever they want control. They pray controlling prayers from an unclean heart and impure motives. The difference in them and a practicing witch is they are professing a hope in Christ but are still operating in carnal and fleshy ways to accomplish their purposes and not God's. They can be delivered if they repent and turn. Otherwise they fall deeper into witchcraft and open themselves up to demonisation. A person with the spirit of a witch will usually be disobedient and rebellious toward pastoral authority. The will seek to destroy relationships and church unity over time and sow seeds of discord and division. They go from church to church never repenting but destroying others and leaving behind their seeds of destruction. You can acquire the spirit of a witch in your life when you have a lot of mixture, been part of a lot of religions, lots of churches, lots of affiliations, lots of broken marriages, lots of false doctrine and lots of false prophecies spoken over you. They can be delivered if they repent and begin to deal with their destructive behaviors laced in rebellion.

Witchcraft- The working together of spirits of rebellion to manipulate supernatural forces to cause harm and damage to people and especially the Kingdom of God. It is also considered a false religion or ancient form of nature religion that uses psychic power through fertility rituals, occult arts, magic and sorcery. Sometimes the religion of witchcraft if referred to today as "The Craft", or "Neopaganism". All witchcraft practices are forbidden by scripture as in Deuteronomy 18:9-14.

Wizard or Warlock- A male practioner of advanced magical arts, like unto a
female witch. An unbeliever, an agent of Satan, who is dedicated to working
the occult arts and is set against the Lord Jesus Christ and His Kingdom.
Can be a male that was dedicated at birth to lord Satan by their parents or
ancestors.

Yin Yang- Comes from the Middle Eastern forces of Taoism. Yin refers to the
passive, negative, females cosmic element, whereas the Yang refers to the active,
positive, masculine cosmic element. The Taoists of ancient China believed
in the existence of an energy called Ch'i. They believed it flowed through the
universe and thorugh invisible energy lines in the human body and organs
(called meridians), this energy was claimed to be controlled by the Yin and the
Yang, two opposing yet harmonizing forces which represent light and dark,
male and female, good and evil. If an imbalance occurs, then sickness or illness
results. It is grounded in alternative therapies and points to the occult.

Yoga- Yoga means "to join." It is a Middle Eastern occult activity masked in
exercise and good health but actually is the entry way for "serpent power" or
Kundalini to absorb a person into universal oneness with the spirit of Buddha
or Hindu spirits. The individual's identity is lost in a type of selfless Nirvana
and they become one with false gods.

APPENDIX F

Suggested Reading List for Pastor's Wives, Ministers Wives and Women in Ministry

Buckingham, Jamie, <u>Daughter of Destiny, Kathryn Kuhlman, Her Story,</u> Gwent, UK, Valley Books, 1976.

Carter, Weptanomah W., <u>The Black Minister's Wife</u>, Ministry of Books, Baltimore, Maryland, 1990.

Claiborne, Minnie, <u>Women in Ministry, How to Be a Winner</u>, Shippenburg, Pa., Companion Press, 1983.

Demarest, Victoria Booth- <u>Sex and Spirit; God, Woman and Ministry</u>, Florida: Valknrie Press, 1977.

Grady, J. Lee, 25 tough Questions About Women and the Church, Charisma House, Lake Mary, Florida, 2003.

Grady, J. Lee, <u>10 Lies the Church Tells Women</u>, Charisma House, Lake Mary, Florida, 2006.

Green, Dr. Jackie L. <u>The Hurt Lady, Spiritual Warfare Manual for the Preacher's Wife</u>, (With Special Sections for Women in Ministry) Author House Publishers, Bloomington, Indiana, 2008.

Green, Dr. Jackie L. <u>My Prince Charming is Abusing Me</u>, JGM-National PrayerLife Institute, Phoenix, AZ 2008.

Green, Dr. Jackie L., <u>When She Hears the Call, Reconciliation in the Pulpit and the Pews</u>, Phoenix, AZ, JGM-National PrayerLife Institute, 1995.

Green, Dr. Jackie L. <u>Spurned into Apostleship, Overcoming Principalities, Powers</u>

and People to Fulfill Destiny, Bloomington, Indiana, Author House Publishers, 2006.

Green, Dr. Jackie L. Women as Bishops, Understanding the Ministry of the Overseer, Phoenix, Arizona, JGM-National PrayerLife Institute, 2006.

Godwin, Rick, Exploring Witchcraft in the Church. Charisma House, Lake Mary Florida, 1997.

Hosier, Helen Kooiman, 100 Christian Women Who Changed the 20th Century, Revell Books, 2000.

Hunter, Fannie McDowell, Women Preachers, Kentucky: Berachah Printing, 1905.

Jacobs, Cindy, Women of Destiny, Ventura, CA, Regal Books, 1998.

Jacobs, Joy, They Were Women, Too., A Daily Devotional based On the Women of the Old Testament, Christian Publications, Camp Hill, PA, 1981.

McKenzie, Bishop Vashti, M., Not Without A Struggle, Leadership Development for A Woman in Ministry., Cleveland, OH, United Church Press, OH, 1996.

McPherson, Aimee Semple, The Story of My Life- Waco, Texas, Word Books, 1973.

Miles, Al Reverend. Domestic Violence-What Every Pastor Needs to Know, Augsburg Fortress Press, Minneapolis, OH, 2000.

Mitchell, Ed., Ella Pearson, Those Preaching Women, Volume I, Valley Forge, Pennsylvania, Judson Press, 1985.

Mitchell, Ed., Ella Pearson, Those Preaching Women, Volume II, Valley Forge, Pennsylvania, Judson Press, 1988.

Mitchell, Ed., Ella Pearson, Women: To Preach or Not to Preach, Valley Forge, Pennsylvania, Judson Press, 1991.

Noren, Carol M., The Woman in the Pulpit, Abingdon Press, Nashville, TN, 1992.

Ross, Charlotte, Who Is the Minister's Wife? The Westminister Press, Philadelphia, 1980.

Truman, Ruth., Underground Manual for Minister's Wives, Abingdon Press, Nashville, Tennessee, 1974.

Wentroble, Barbara, Rise to Our Destiny Woman of God, Regal Books, Ventura,

CA, 2006.

White, Ruthe, <u>What Every Pastor's Wife Should Know</u>, Tyndale House Publishers, Wheaton, Illinois, 1987.

Williams, Pat and Ruth, How to be Like Women of Influence, Health Communications, Inc., Deerfield Beach, Florida, 2003.

Wilson, Frank and P. Bunny, <u>The Master's Degree, Majoring in Your Marriage</u>, Harvest House Publishers, Eugene, Oregon, 1996.

Suggested Reading List for Spiritual Growth

Alec, Wendy, *Journal of the Unknown Prophet*, Warboys Media, 2005.

Baer, Randall, *Inside the New Age Nightmare*, Huntington House, Inc., Layfayette, LA, 1989.

Barclay, Mark, *Sheep, Goats and Wolves*, Mark Barclay Ministries, 1985.

Barna, George, *What You Need to Know About Today's Youth*, Regal Books, Ventura, California, 1995.

Bernal, Dick, *America Spiritually Mapped*, Jubilee Christian Center, San Jose, CA, 1994.

Blumhofer, Edith L., *Aimee Semple McPherson, Everybody's Sister*, William B. Edermans Publishing, Grand Rapids, Michigan, 1993.

Burns, Cathy Dr., *Hidden Secrets of the Eastern Star*, Sharing Publishing, Mt. Carmel, PA, 1994.

Chavda, Mahesh & Bonnie, *Watch of the Lord*, Creation House, Lake Mary, Florida, 1999.

Clark, Jonas, *Seducing Goddess of War*, Spirit of Life Ministries, Ft. Lauderdale, FL., 2001.

Conner, Kevin, *The Church in the New Testament*, B.T. Publishing, Portland, Oregon, 1982.

Cooke, Graham, *Developing Your Prophetic Gifting*, Sovereign World, England, 1994.

Crawford, Beverly Bam, Private Collection Tapes; Bible Enrichment Seminars, *Women in Ministry, Free from Fear*, Parts I and II, Inglewood, CA 1988.

Damazio, Frank, *The Gate Church*, City Bible Publishing, Portland, Oregon, 2000.

Damazio, Frank, *The Making of a Leader*, B.T. Publishing, Portland, Oregon, 1988.

Daniels, Kimberly, *Against All Odds*, Spread the Word Publishing, Jacksonville, FL, 2000.

Daniels, Kimberly, *Clean House, Strong House*, (*A Practical Guide to Understanding Spiritual Warfare*), Charisma House, Lake Mary, Florida, 2003.

Daniels, Kimberly, *From a Mess to a Miracle*, Creation House Press, Lake Mary, Florida, 2002.

Delbridge, Deborah D., *Diseases of the Soul, Confronting Hidden Issues of the Heart*, Creation House Press, Lake Mary, Florida, 2003.

Eastman, Dick and Hayford, Jack, *Living and Praying In Jesus' Name*, Tyndale House, Wheaton, IL, 1988.

Eberyl, Harold R., *The Complete Wineskin*, (*Restructuring the Church for the Outpouring of the Holy Spiri)t*, Winepress Publishing, 1989.

Eckhardt, John, *Apostles or Bishops?*, Crusaders Ministries, Oak Park/Chicago, IL, 2004.

Eckhardt, John, *Demon Hit List*, Whitaker House, New Kensington, PA, 1995.

Eckhardt, John, *Moving in the Apostolic*, Renew Publishing, Ventura, CA, 1999.

Eckhardt, John, *50 Truths Concerning Apostolic Ministry*, Crusaders Ministries, Chicago, IL, 1994.

Engle, Lou, Digging the Wells of Revival, Revival Press, Shippenburg, PA, 1998.

Woodworth-Etter, Mary, *Signs and Wonders*, Whitaker Hall, Kensington, CA 1997.

Fletcher, Kingsley, *I Have Seen the Kingdom*, A Revelation of God's Final Glory, Creation House, Orlando, Florida, 1998.

Gentile, Ernest, *Your Sons and Daughters Shall Prophesy*, Chosen Books, Grand Rapids, Michigan, 1999.

Gibson, Noel and Phyl, *Evicting Demonic Intruders*, New Wine Press, West Sussex, England, 1993.

Gibson, Noel and Phyl, *Excuse Me Your Rejection is Showing*, Sovereign World, Kent, England, 1992.

Goll, James W., *Praying for Israel's Destiny*, Chosen Books, Grand Rapids, MI,

2005.

Goll, James, *The Seer*, Destiny Image Publishers, Shippensburg, PA, 2004.

Grant, Bernard, *First Class Leaders*, Fifty Principles for Becoming a Strong Leader, Milestones International Publishers, 2004.

Hamon, Bill, *Apostles, Prophets and the Coming Move of God*, Christian International, Santa, Rosa, CA 1997.

Hammond, Frank and Ida Mae, *Pigs in the Parlor*, A Practical Guide to Deliverance, Impact Books, Kirkwood, MD 1973.

Hammond, Frank and Ida Mae, *Our Warfare Against Demons and Territorial Spirits,* The Children's Bread Ministry, Plainview, TX, 1991.

Hammond, Frank and Ida Mae, *Children's Deliverance*, Impact Christian Books, Kirkwood, MD, 1996

Harris, Jack, *Freemasonry*, Whitaker House, New Kensington, PA, 1936.

Harari, Oren, *The Leadership Secrets of Colin Powell*, McGraw Hill Publishers, NY,NY, 2002.

Hendricks, William & Howard, *Building Character in a Mentoring Relationship As Iron Sharpens Iron*, Moody Press, Chicago, IL, 1995.

Herzog, David, *Desperate for New Wine*, Sovereign World, Kent, England, 1997.

Hosier, Helen Kooiman, *100 Christian Women Who Changed the 20th Century*, Revell, A Division of Baker Books House Co.,

Haugk, Kenneth C. *Antagonists in the Church, How to Identify and Deal with Destructive Conflict*, Augsburg Publishing House, 1988.

Hopkins, Apostle Ivory, *Deliverance from Evil Soul Ties*, A Handbook for Breaking Difficult Bondages Related to Soul Ties, Royal Creations, Harbeson, DE.

Hopkins, Apostle Ivory, *Deliverance from Marriage Breaking Spirits*, Pilgrims Ministry of Deliverance, Harbeson, DE.

Hopkins, Apostle Ivory, *Deliverance from Damaged Emotions*, Royal Creation, Harbeson, DE, 2000.

Hopkins, Apostle Ivory, *Deliverance from The Draining Spirit*, Royal Creation, 1998.

Illnisky, Esther, *Let the Children Pray, How God's Young Intercessors are Changing the World*, Regal Books, Ventura, CA 2000.

Jacobs, Cindy, *Women of Destiny*, Regal Books, 1998.

Jacobs, Cindy, *Deliver Us From Evil*, Putting A Stop to the Occult Influences Invading Your Home and Community Regal Books, Ventura, CA, 2001.

Jakes, Bishop T.D., *Woman, Thou Art Loosed*, Healing the Wounds of the Past, Treasure House, Shippenburg, PA, 1993.

Joyner, Rick, *Overcoming Racism*, Morning Star Publications, Charlotte, NC, 1996.

Joyner, Rick, *Overcoming the Religious Spirit, Combating Spiritual Strongholds Series*, Morning Star Publications, Charlotte, NC, 1996.

Joyner, Rick, *Overcoming Witchcraft*, Morning Star Publications, NC, 1996.

Kelly, John with Costa, Paul, *End Time Warriors*, Renew Books, Ventura, CA, 1999.

King, D.E., *Preaching to Preachers*, Neibauer Press, Warminster, PA, 1984.

Kreider, Larry, *The Cry for Spiritual Father's and Mothers*, House to House Publications, Ephrata, PA, 2000.

Koch, Kurt, *Occult Bondage and Deliverance*, Kregel Publishers, Grand Rapids, MI, 1970.

Lardie, Debra, *Concise Dictionary of the Occult and New Age*, Kregel, Pub, Grand Rapid, MI, 2000.

Layton, Dian, *Soldiers with Little Feet*, Destiny Image Pub., Shippensberg, PA 1989.

Liardon, Roberts, *Breaking Controlling Powers*, Albury Publishing, Tulsa, OK, 1991.

Liardon, Roberts, *Sharpen Your Discernment*, Albury Publishing, Tulsa, OK, 1997.

Lockyer, Herbert, *All the Men of the Bible*, Zondervan, Grand Rapids, MI, 1958.

Lockyer, Herbert, *All the Women of the Bible*, Zondervan, Grand Rapids, MI, 1958.

MacNutt, Francis, *Deliverance From Evil Spirits, A Practical Manual*.

Malkmus, Rev. George, *Why Christians Get Sick*, Treasure House, Shippensburg, PA, 1989.

Milligan, Ira, *Understanding The Dreams You Dream*, Treasure House, Shippensburg, PA, 1997.

Morgan, Dr. Patricia, *How to Raise Children of Destiny*, Destiny Image, Shippensburg, Publishers, 1994.

Munroe, Dr. Myles, *Power of Vision, Principles and Keys*, Whitaker House. Chicago Heights, Chicago, 2000.

Salem, Harry and Cheryl, *Distraction from Destiny, Eight Distractions You Must Overcome*, Harrison House, Tulsa, OK, 2001. (Salem Family Ministries)

Servello, Pastor Mike, *God's Shield of Protection*, Mt. Zion Ministries, 2003.

Smith, Alice, *Beyond the Veil, God's Call to Intimate Intercession*, SpiriTruth Publishing, Houston, Texas, 1996.

Thompson, Dr. Millicent, *Don't Die in the Winter, Your Season Is Coming*, Treasure House, Shippensburg, PA, 1995.

Peretti, Frank, *The Wounded Spirit*, Word Publishing, 2000.

Pierce, Chuck D. and Sytsema, Rebecca, *Possessing Your Inheritance*, Renew Books, 1999.

Pierce, Chuck, D., and Sytsema, Rebecca W., *Receiving the Word of the Lord, Bringing Life to Your Prophetic Word*, Wagner Institute for Practical Ministry, Colorado Springs, CO, 1999.

Pierce, Chuck D. and Sytsema, Rebecca, *The Best is Yet Ahead*, Wagner Publication, Colorado Springs, CO, 2001.

Pierce, Chuck D. and Sheets, Dutch, *Releasing the Prophetic Destiny of A Nation*, Destiny Image Publishers, Inc., Shippensburg, PA, 2005.

Pierce, Chuck D. and Sytsema, Rebecca, *The Future War of the Church*, Regal Books, Ventura, CA 2001.

Price, Kenneth, *The Eagle Christian*, Old Faithful Publishing Co., Wetumpka, AL, 1984.

Powell, Colin, *Leadership Secrets of Colin Powell*, McGraw Publishers, 2003.

Trimm, Dr. Cindy, *The Rules of Engagement, Book I and II,* Cindy Trimm, Corporation Ft. Lauderdale, Florida, Strang Communications, 2005.

Vallowe, Ed. F. *Biblical Mathematics, Keys to Scripture Numerics*, Vallowe Evang. Association, Forest Park, GA< 1991.

Wagner, Doris, M. *How to Cast Out Demons, A Guide to Basics*, Renew Books, Ventura, CA, 2000.

Wagner, C. Peter, Editor, *Territorial Spirits*, Sovereign World Limited, England, 1991.

Wagner, C. Peter, *Prayer Shield, How to Intercede for Pastors, Christian Leaders and others on the Frontlines* (The Prayer Warrior Series), Regal Books, Ventura, CA 1992.

Wentroble, Apostle Barbara, *Prophetic Intercession*, Renew Books, Ventura, CA, 1999.

Wilkinson, Bruce, The Dream Giver, Multnomah Publishers, Sisters, Oregon, 2003.

Williams, Prophet Connie, *The Woman Side of God*, End Time Wave Publications, Bogota, NJ, 1998.

Worley, Win, *Witchcraft Workings in the Church*, Win Worley Publications, Mesquite, TX, 1990.

Worley, Win, *Rooting Out Rejection and Hidden Bitterness*, Win Worley Publications, 1992.

Worley, Win, *Conquering the Host of Hell*, Win Worley Publications, 1981.

Worley, Win, *Annihilating the Host of Hell*, Book I, Win Worley Publications, 1981.

ABOUT THE AUTHOR

Bishop Dr. Jackie L. Green is an apostle set in the Body of Christ to bring reformation, revelation and reconciliation. She is married to Pastor Anthony Green, where they have pastored the Second Baptist Church of Redlands, California for over 20 years, and been married for 35 years, with four young adult children and two grandchildren, and many spiritual sons and daughters. They minister together teaching Kingdom Marriages retreats and couple's fellowships as counselors and group leaders for clergy and Christian couples. Dr. Green is founder and Senior Pastor of the New Generation Christian Fellowship Church of Phoenix, Arizona. She is the Executive Minister and Founder of JGM-National PrayerLife Institute, a covering ministry for several apostolic and prophetic ministries. She continues to be a spiritual mentor and midwife for women in the wilderness of their calling; five fold ministers, and pastoral families. She is an author and biblical scholar, bringing an upgrade to the "prayer life of America," offering fresh new curriculum and prayer education resources. She received her B.A. Degree from the State University of New York, her M.A. Degree from Fuller Theological Seminary of Pasadena, and Doctor of Practical Ministry Degree from Wagner Leadership Institute, Colorado, Springs, Colorado. Bishop Green has numerous books and materials available through her ministry and websites. She and her family reside in Redlands, California and Phoenix, Arizona.

Printed in the United States
216725BV00002B/5/P